Masonic Trivia

With Best Wishes
Allen E Roberts

Frontispiece to "Ahiman Rezon," 1764.

The title "Ahiman Rezon" is derived from three Hebrew words, אחים, *ahim*, "brothers," מנה, *manah*, "to appoint," or "to select," and רצון, *ratzon*, "the will, pleasure or meaning;" and hence the combination of the three words in the title, Ahiman Rezon, signifies "the will of selected brethren" = the law of a class or society of men who are chosen or selected from the rest of the world as brethren.

Masonic Trivia (and Facts)

Allen E. Roberts

Anchor Communications
Highland Springs, Virginia

Copyright (c) 1994 by Allen E. Roberts

All rights reserved. No part of this book may be reproduced or translated in any form or by any means without the written permission of the publisher.

Anchor Communications
PO Box 70
Highland Springs, Virginia 23075

ISBN-0-935633-14-6

Manufactured in the United States of America

Dedicated

To those who seek the light of truth and those who spread this truth, especially The Masonic Service Association and The Philalethes Society that have been enlightening the Masonic world for three-fourths of a century; and to Dottie.

Books By Allen E. Roberts

House Undivided: The Story of Freemasonry and the Civil War
Freemasonry in Highland Springs
A Daughter of the Grand Lodge of Virginia
Sword and Trowel: The story of Military Lodges
Masonry Under Two Flags
Key to Freemasonry's Growth
How to Conduct a Successful Leadership Seminar
Freemasonry's Servant: The History of the MSA
Fifty Golden Years: The History of Warwick Lodge
Brotherhood in Action!: The History of the Virginia Craftsmen
The Craft and Its Symbols
G. Washington: Master Mason
Frontier Cornerstone: The History of the Grand Lodge of Ohio
Shedding Light on Leadership
A Chronicle of Virginia Research Lodge
Freemasonry in American History
Who is Who in Freemasonry (2 editions)
Brother Truman
La Francmasoneria Y Sus Simbolos (Spanish version of
    The Craft and Its Symbols)
The Diamond Years: Seventy-five Year History of Babcock Lodge
The Search For Leadership
Seekers of Truth
The Mystic Tie
Masonic Lifeline: Leadership
   Several books revised for Macoy Publishing & Masonic Supply Co.

Award-winning Motion Pictures by Allen E. Roberts

The Pilot	*The Brotherhood of Man...*
Growing the Leader	*Challenge!*
Breaking Barriers to Communication	*Precious Heritage*
Planning Unlocks the Door	*Lonely World*
People Make the Difference	*"Fraternally Yours"*
Virtue Will Triumph	*Living Stones...*

The Connecting Link
The Saga of the Holy Royal Arch of Freemasonry

Foreword

I am flattered to be asked to contribute a few preliminary remarks to the latest book by Allen E. Roberts.

It's a risky business when one reaches the age of "maturity." There's an awful tendency to repeat what you have been saying over the years. But never mind! If it's true, it won't hurt to repeat it. And so I tell you once again, education has always been one of the main functions of Freemasonry. To be sure, its degrees and certificates are not recognized in the profane world as marks of achievement. But the opportunity is there.

Now, let's be clear about one thing. There are problems involved in the process. When I was a young Mason, as I said a while ago, "I used to listen to what was called 'Masonic education.' You know the sort of thing: awkward demonstrations of the wrong way to give the signs; boring lectures about Brotherly Love, Relief and Truth; grotesque sermons on the moral lessons to be drawn from the Heavy Setting Maul; rambling travelogues on the Great Pyramids of Egypt; mystical ravings based on the Pythagorean Theorem; shallow discussions of the meaning of the word 'Landmarks'; the story of the first twenty-five years of a lodge nobody ever heard of; the life of some guy from a century ago who never did anything worthwhile. None of this was very exciting, but it seemed to be what Masons did, and so I listened patiently. I was a Mason for over fifteen years before anyone told me that someone had actually written a book on Masonry."

This underlines one of the main difficulties associated with Masonic education. If you're going to do a good job, you have to have access to reliable and well-written information. There are good books, and there are bad books. And once you begin to browse, you will keep on bumping into one Masonic writer that you can depend on. And now Allen E. Roberts has done it again.

But is it really necessary to say anything about him? Does he need any introduction? Is there anyone out there who hasn't heard of him?

America has never had such a productive Masonic author, such a dynamic Masonic communicator, such an effective Masonic educator, such a clear-sighted Masonic advisor as Allen Roberts. So many of his books ought to be in the hands of every thoughtful Brother! He is a true hero to many of us, all over the free world. We all owe a tremendous debt to him; he has done so much for the gentle Craft.

His hard work and his talents are beginning to be recognized in high places. It is entirely appropriate that on July 9, 1994, to celebrate the achievements of Right Worshipful Allen Earl Roberts, Most Worshipful Thomas Frederick May, Grand Master of Masons in the Commonwealth of Virginia, officiated at a ceremony in which the Grand Lodge renamed its library and museum in honor of this Masonic author and educator.

Now here, in these pages, Allen has once again produced a work that will be of interest to every thoughtful Mason. Once again he has allowed me to see it, chapter by chapter, as it was written. Clear, instructive, historically accurate, inspiring, wide-ranging — these are the words that leaped to mind as I went through it.

We are so lucky that he is still producing educational material, at an age when many of us have been forced out to pasture. Keep up the good work, Allen!

> Wallace McLeod
> *Past Grand Senior Warden* (Canada, Ontario)
> *Professor of Classics*, U. of Toronto

Festival of St. John the Baptist
24 June 1994

Preface

The problem in writing this volume was in deciding what to ignore, not what should be included! It was an almost impossible task. Here I have tried to ask and answer some of the questions most often asked over the years.

Many histories and other books have been consulted in order to provide the facts that the reader will find in this work. Many of them are listed in the Bibliography. But if I was asked to recommend just one book for further study of early Freemasonry, it would be *The Grand Design* by Wallace McLeod. McLeod is a Masonic historian and researcher without equal. His book contains the vital substance, briefly, of the better historians of yesteryear.

I would strongly recommend that anything written prior to the past fifty years be consulted with caution. Earlier writers did little serious research. Many of them were careless with facts. Many of these untruths have been kept alive by well-meaning Masonic speakers, editors and writers. Too many of these have furnished fuel for the pugnacity of anti-Masonic zealots.

Why no footnotes? Because almost every answer to every question would require several! When I wrote the manuscript of *House Undivided* I found I had to consult at least three accounts of every battle, historical and Masonic event, to try to determine the truth. Historians are supposed to be unbiased — few are. I wanted the reader to be able to say that the story of Freemasonry during the Civil War **was** unbiased. I'm told I achieved that goal. I must confess, however, that I had to tear up dozens of pages of manuscript to make it so.

Another account of footnotes is found in an article written in June 1993 by Theo Lippman, Jr. titled "Lawyers Paid by the Colon?" About footnotes he claimed: "One purpose of the footnote in law reviews is to show agreement with the author's point. Another is to make sure you get it. Footnotes often include lengthy explanations of what the text means and what the footnote means. And another purpose of law review footnotes is to demonstrate to the reader that the writer has read widely. So the more the merrier." He also notes, as I have on many occasions, that some articles contain more footnotes than original text! I found many years ago that far too often footnotes contain erroneous information. These are a few of the reasons I abhor them.

Let me inject at this point that I must offer a defense of my statements in chapter nine concerning General George B. McClellan. I fully realize my admiration of him isn't shared by many historians (or so-called historians). Most people are convinced President Abraham Lincoln was infallible, always told the truth, and never could do anything wrong. Lincoln's apologists have seen to this.

Among the sources I have relied on is the *History of the Fifth Regiment, New Hampshire Volunteers,* in which we learn about Colonel Edward E. Cross (a New Hampshire Freemason), commanding officer of the regiment. He continually led his men into the thick of the fighting. Based on what I have learned about Cross, he was a brilliant military tactician, a man who searched for truth, remarkably patriotic, out-spoken, and far too exceptional to please the Federal war department.

Cross first met McClellan on November 26, 1861. He had fought with and for him, and this would continue. When President Lincoln first fired McClellan in November 1862, Cross wrote in his personal journal: "Here we heard of the removal of McClellan from command of the army—at this time an ill-advised operation. We were going on well, and two days more would have brought us to the enemy."

Concerning the Federal debacle at Fredericksburg, Virginia, Cross wrote in his report: "Hooker has not the amount of brains necessary to manage a vast army. In generalship we fall far behind the rebels, and since McClellan left the Army of the Potomac its organization has been extremely defective.... [Hooker's] failure was predicted by thousands of officers and soldiers, from the first day he started." Only Lincoln had any confidence in Hooker (in whose "honor" lewd females have ever since been dubbed), helping to prove the President knew little about military tactics.

Just before the battle at Antietam, Federal troops were forced to retreat from Centreville. Cross wrote: "... after covering the withdrawal of that humbug, General Pope, who came near ruining the Federal cause, McClellan was sent for to save the army." With Lee's army threatening Maryland, Cross said: "The prospect was dark indeed; but the emergency roused the President to act on his own responsibility. He sent for General McClellan and tendered him the command of the army for the defence of the Capitol. Pope was sent off to the frontier."

Cross had been severely wounded several times. During the Battle of Gettysburg he was mortally wounded. His body was carried to New Hampshire where his Lodge conducted his funeral.

If your appetite is whetted for in depth information on any subject found herein, check out the volumes listed in the bibliography. They are among the best accounts on their subjects to be found.

Two men have made this to be more historically and grammatically correct than it would otherwise have been: Wallace E. McLeod, a professor at Victoria College in Ontario, and Richard E. Fletcher, Executive Secretary of The Masonic Service Association. My appreciation to them knows no bounds. Bear in mind, however, that any mistakes are mine alone.

Allen E. Roberts

Highland Springs, Virginia
July 4, 1994

Contents

Frontispiece.. *ii*
Foreword... *vii*
Preface.. *ix*

1. In the Beginning.. 1
2. The Grand Lodge Era Begins............................. 13
3. Freemasonry in Early North America............... 29
4. Forming a Republic... 41
5. The Influence of George Washington................ 55
6. Growth of American Freemasonry..................... 65
7. Bigots Ferociously Malign the Craft................. 73
8. Freemasonry Moves Forward.............................. 79
9. The Undivided Craft... 87
10. Shambles and Shame... 101
11. Westward... 109
12. War and Brotherhood.. 117
13. War (Again) and Homes Away From Home... 129
14. After the War.. 139
15. Onward.. 151
16. Toward the Next Century................................... 159
17. Potpourri.. 169

About the Author.. 181
Bibliography... 183
Index.. 187

Masonic Trivia (and Facts)

1. In the Beginning

It has been well said "that we must despair of ever being able to reach the fountainhead of streams which have been running and increasing from the beginning of time. All that we can aspire to do is only to trace their course backward, as far as possible, on these charts that now remain of the distant countries whence they were first perceived to flow." It has also to be borne in mind that as all trustworthy history must necessarily be a work of compilation, the imagination of the writer must be held in subjection. He can but use and shape his materials, and these unavoidably will take a somewhat fragmentary form.
                                                Robert Freke Gould

1. When did Freemasonry begin?

No one knows when Freemasonry began. The first written reference to Masonry as an organization appeared in 1356 when a Code of Mason Regulations was formally drawn up at the Guildhall in London, England. In 1376 we find information about the London Masons' Company and it's interesting to note its early evolution. According to *Grand Lodge*, it leased in 1463 some land and buildings for 99 years, and the buildings were converted into the first Masons' Hall. (In the 99th year it purchased this property outright); in 1472 the company was given a Grant of Arms with the motto "God Is Our Guide," later changed to "In the Lord is all our trust." The Arms, but slightly changed, remain part of the Arms of the United Grand Lodge of England today.

2. What is the *Regius Manuscript*?

The first known document about Freemasonry.

3. Who determined the *Regius Manuscript* (or *Poem*) to be what it is?

   A non-Mason named J.O. Halliwell-Phillips (the Phillips was added much later to appease his father-in-law).

4. How was the *Regius Manuscript* first cataloged?

   As "A Manuscript of Moral Duties."

5. Where was and is the original copy of the *Regius Manuscript* kept?

   In the British Library. (Its early history is unknown, but it apparently belonged at one time to John Thomas. The first known owner of record was John Thayer, an antiquarian who died in 1673; his grandmother Ann Hart Theyer offered his library to Bodlia Library at Oxford University, but it didn't accept it, so it was sold to Robert Scott, a London book dealer, then it was sold to Charles II after 1678 [the volume was valued at two shillings!]; it eventually became a part of the Royal Library (thus the name "Regius" attached to the manuscript), and in 1757 the library was presented to the British Museum by George II in whose honor the collection is known as "The Regius Collection.")

6. When was the *Regius Manuscript* discovered to be a poem about Freemasonry?

   In 1839. Halliwell presented a paper on this manuscript in that year; a portion of the paper was published in *Archaeologia* in 1840; in the same year the poem was reprinted, and has been many times since then.

7. In what language is the *Regius Manuscript* written? What year was it written?

   It was written about A.D. 1390, and was evidently copied from an older document. It is written in Middle English making it difficult for the non-linguist to decipher. Over the years several linguists have translated it into modern English.

8. Is any of the *Regius Poem* followed today in the ritual of Freemasonry?

Indeed it is followed. A reading of the poem will reveal many areas in which Freemasonry still advocates the performance of the moral duties advocated in the *Regius Manuscript*. "So Mote It Be," meaning "So May It Be," is an example of a phrase that is still recited constantly by Freemasons.

9. According to the *Regius Manuscript* who called an assembly of all masons to meet? Where? When?

Athelstan (925-940), virtually King of all England, according to the *Regius Manuscript*, called the masons to meet, then he gave them "modernized" charges and sent them forth to carry them out. James Anderson said this took place at York, England, in 926. Coil notes that the two earliest documents (the *Regius* and *Cooke*) don't mention York, and he believes the date would be closer to 932. Perhaps the best known portion of the *Regius* is found in lines 61 to 66 which read:
The Craft came into England, as I now say,
In the time of good King Athelstán's day;
He made them both hall and likewise bower
And high Temples of great honor,
To disport him in both day and night,
And to worship his God with all his might.

10. How many theories can be found about the beginnings of Freemasonry?

At least 25 theories of Freemasonry's beginning were prevalent for many years, according to Henry Wilson Coil. (He developed these from the writings of Gould.) These included: 1. King Solomon; 2. The Temple of Solomon; 3. Euclid; 4. Pythagoras; 5. The creation of the world; 6. The Patriarchal Religion; 7. Moses; 8. The ancient pagan mysteries; 9. The Essenes; 10. The Culdees; 11. The Druids; 12. The Gypsies; 13. The Rosicrucians; 14. The Crusades; 15. The Knights Templar; 16. Oliver Cromwell; 17. The Pretender for the Restoration of the House of Stuart; 18. Lord Bacon; 19. Dr. Desaguliers and his associates in 1717; 20. The Roman Collegia of Artificers; 21. The Comacine Masters; 22. The Steinmetzen; 23. The French Compagnons; 24. Sir Christopher Wren at the building of St. Paul's Cathedral; 25. The English and Scots operative Freemasons of the Middle Ages. Most of these theories have been discounted by creditable historians. (This will become evident later.)

11. Who, in the opinion of most historians, was the foremost Masonic historian who compiled an account of the earlycenturies in the development of the Craft?

Robert Freke Gould. His three volume *The History of Freemasonry*, written between 1882 and 1887, painstakingly covers the history of the Craft from what is known about its beginning through 1885. Gould was made a Freemason in Royal Navy Lodge No. 429 in Ramsgate while he was stationed with the British army in East Kent in 1854. He served as Master of several Lodges, including Quatuor Coronati No. 2076 as its second Master. He received many honors throughout the world, but it was a little over a year before his death that the United Grand Lodge of England recognized his greatness and contributions to Freemasonry. It then created him a Past Grand Warden.

12. Where are the earliest lodge records to be found in Scotland? In England? Who were some non-operative Masons?

In Scotland the earliest lodge records still in existence were recorded in a Lodge at Aitchison's Haven in 1598; minutes of Mary's Chapel lodge at Edinburgh are unbroken from 1599, and within the pages is a copy, in Schaw's own hand, is a set of his Statutes of 1598. In England, according to Gould, only the records of Alnwick between the dates of 1700 and 1717 are known to have been recorded. *Grand Lodge* tells us: "Early evidence relating to other [than Acception] non-operative Lodges is very scarce." *The Grand Lodge of Scotland Year Book* claims that King James VI and I were admitted to Lodge Scoon and Perth in 1601; and Sir Robert Moray was initiated at Newcastle in 1641. From many sources we learn of Elias Ashmole's entry on October 16, 1646 in his diary: "I was made a Free-Mason at Warrenton in Lancashire" along with "Coll: Henry Mainwaring of Karincham in Cheshire." He added the names of seven members of the lodge. The records of this lodge have disappeared.

13. When did Freemasonry enter Ireland?

No one knows. It was some time after a Grand Lodge was formed in England before the first Lodge came into being in Ireland. Without doubt Masonry was known there at least as early as July 11, 1688. Coil records a speech by one John Jones at a commencement in the University of Dublin:

It was lately ordered that for the honor and dignity of the University there should be introduced a Society of Freemasons, consisting of gentlemen, mechanics, porters, parsons, ragmen, hucksters, divines, tinkers, knights, thatchers, cobblers, poets, justices, drawers, beggars, aldermen, paviours, sculls, freshmen, bachelors, scavingers, masters, sawgelders, doctors, ditchers, pimps, lords, butchers, and tailors, who shall bind themselves by an oath never to discover their mighty no-secret; and to relieve whatsoever strolling distress brethren they meet with, after the example of the Fraternity of Freemasons in and about Trinity College, by whom a collections was lately made for, and the purse of charity well stuffed for, a reduced Brother, who received their charity as follows....

The learned gentleman, undoubtedly intending to be sarcastic, told us volumes about Freemasonry. It was composed of all types of men who were considered for their inward qualities, not their worldly wealth or honors. They were practicing charity. They had a ritual, which, evidently even then, was "no-secret."

14. Which *Gothic* or *Manuscript Constitutions* (hereafter called *Gothic*) contained the first link between the Craft and King Solomon's Temple?

The *Cooke Manuscript* of 1410. Harry Carr in *Grand Lodge* recorded this from this Manuscript: "And at the making of Solomon's Temple that King David began   King David loved all Masons, and he gave them charges right nigh as they are now. And at the making of the Temple in Solomon's time, as it is said in the Bible, in III Book of Kings ... that Solomon had four score thousand Masons at his work; and the King's son of Tyre was his Master Mason." (See also Q. 33.)

15. "Time Immemorial" is used frequently in Freemasonry; what does it mean?

Other explanations are given, but briefly "Time Immemorial" can be termed as ancient, something having existed from a time one cannot remember. Examples of this will be found later.

16. A major group of historians believe Freemasonry descended from stonemasons. How long have these craftsmen been in existence?

It is generally agreed that stonemasons, in some form, have existed all over the world since the dawn of time, long before the building of the pyramids in Egypt. Actually it takes no stretch of the imagination to realize there had to be stone masons, and other craftsmen, since men first began to build edifices to protect them from the elements. This would require some type of organizing leading to some type of organization. Stories in the Bible and other old historical documents readily verify this theory.

17. How long have lodges with speculative masons been in existence?

To be historically accurate, one cannot go beyond six centuries to find lodges of masons accepting men other than operative craftsmen. And for many centuries few, other than actual craftsmen were accepted. But it's not unreasonable to assume clerics and other educated men were readily united with the craftsmen (most of whom couldn't read or write). *Grand Lodge* says the first record of non-operatives being accepted was in July 1634 when Lord Alexander, Sir Anthony Alexander and Sir Alexander Strachan were admitted "fellow craft" in the Lodge of Edinburgh (Mary's Chapel). Coil dates non operative masons from 1600 in the Lodge of Edinburgh, but McLeod believes this is incorrect. The non-operative, John Boswell, attended a trial of a warden, not a meeting of the Lodge. But this Lodge did admit Lord Alexander of Menstrie in 1634 as a Fellowcraft. Then Coil finds non-operatives in Kelso, 1652; Aberdeen, 1670; Kilwinning, 1672. He found the last of the operative masons as members of a lodge in Lodge Glasgow in 1842.

18. Where did the term "lodge" come from?

As with many things we can only speculate as to where the word "lodge" derived. Dictionaries say that it probably came from the buildings, or huts, where the craftsmen worked and lived. Lodges of masons are men-tioned at York Minster in 1352, at Canterbury Cathedral in 1429, at the Church of St. Nicholas, Aberdeen in 1483, and at St. Giles, Edinburgh, in 1491. "Lodge" first referred to non-permanent bodies, but gradually reverted to fixed localities, such as Edinburgh in 1598.

19. What's the story of "The Four Crown Martyrs" for whom the premier research Lodge (Quatuor Coronati) is named?

Gould recounts the tale in this fashion: In A.D. 298, during the reign of Diocletian, the Roman Emperor, five Christian stone masons refused to carve a statue of a pagan god. They were put to death and cast into the Tiber. Crowns appeared on the water above where the bodies had sunk. (That's **five** crowns!) Two years later the Emperor ordered all soldiers to march past and throw incense on the altar of Aesculapius. Four Christian officers refused to obey the order. They were put to death, and later became the martyrs. So we have **four** of them. Later all nine were honored. In Germany the five became four. In all of the known *Gothic Constitutions* this legend is mentioned only in the *Regius*.

20. How many *Gothic Constitutions* are known to exist?

At least 113, beginning with the *Regius* of c. 1390 and ending with the *Wren* c. 1852. Most follow much the same form: an invocation, legends (mostly the same), charges, and an oath. All are religious and moral in concept. All call for mutual helpfulness.

21. About how much did the early masons earn?

By statute in 1350 a master freestone mason earned eight cents per day; other masons, six cents. In 1445, a freemason received eight cents per day, with food; ten cents without. In Scotland the wages were less. In 1610 there was an increase! It's estimated a mason earned about five times the cost of his board each day. (A personal note: In 1930, a youngster of 12, I worked in a bakery for $1.50 for a seven day week; five days after school, all day Saturdays and Sundays.)

22. What were the **Schaw Statutes**?

In 1598 these statutes, or rules and regulations, were enacted in Scotland to cause the craftsmen to observe the ancient usages and to live charitably together. Fines were made enforceable. Obedience to wardens, deacons and masters was enjoined. Cowans were prevented from working under any master, and other rules and regulations pertaining to craftsmen were made mandatory. In 1599 these statutes were amended at the request of Kilwinning Lodge in an attempt to receive royal recognition. The masters convened at Edinburgh and thirteen articles were adopted. Royal recognition was obtained in part.

23. What is a cowan?

Early on a cowan was termed a man who learned to build walls without mortar. This was done without the benefit of an apprenticeship to the trade and one was not admitted to a lodge. He was called in some circles a "dry-diker." He is defined as "a mason without the word." McLeod, quoting from *Early Masonic Catechisms*, that a Masonic catechism of 1730 asks: "If a cowan (or listener) is catched, how is he to be punished?" Answer: "To be placed under the eaves of the houses (in rainy weather) till the water runs in at his shoulders and out at his shoes."

24. Is Kilwinning Lodge the oldest Lodge in Scotland?

The Schaw Statutes state Kilwinning Lodge was "the head and second lodge of Scotland"; the Lodge at Edinburgh, "the first and principal lodge of Scotland." No attempt was made for years to determine if other Lodges were older, and it would appear there were. For instance, Edinburgh became No. 1 after the formation of the Grand Lodge. Several years later the Lodge of Melrose St. John became No. 1 (bis); and Aberdeen No. 1 (ter). Most importantly, Kilwinning became Mother Kilwinning No. 0 (its antiquity was recognized). Perhaps even more important, *The Grand Lodge of Scotland Year Book* even marked the Lodges that had been chartered by Kilwinning! One Scottish historian reported the number at 35; another writer claimed there were at least seven more, and that the true number would never be known. (In Virginia, Port Royal Kilwinning Crosse received a charter from Kilwinning. This became the original No. 2 on the roster of the Grand Lodge of Virginia.) It might be well to note at this point: Massachusetts determined to by-pass the numbering confusion; it refused to number its Lodges. Virginia, on the other hand, granted No. 1 to a Lodge for which there's no evidence it should be, and by filling in vacant numbers over the years predictable problems developed. The first known Lodge to appear in Virginia was the Lodge at Fredericksburg as a "Time Immemorial Lodge" which eventually received a charter from the Grand Lodge of Scotland.

25. Why was a form of recognition necessary for Freemasons?

While honest differences of opinion abound, it is generally believed the peculiar characteristics of the men called free masons made a form of recognition necessary. The *Old Charges (Gothic Constitutions)* say that masons were charged to help one another. A traveler, if he proved himself a mason, was to be given work if possible.

If no work was available, he was to be given food, housing, and enough money to travel to the next lodge.

26. Why do Freemasons recite "blood curdling" penalties?

Again there is an honest difference of opinion. First it must be emphasized: **These penalties have never been carried out**. It must be remembered that few men could read and write, they had to depend on clerics and other learned men for information. They learned "by mouth to ear." This is one reason the early Masonic catechisms contained so many doublets and triplets such as: duly and truly; worthy and well qualified; conceal, hele (to cover) and never reveal; and so on. The breaking of vows was considered morally foul (and this concept should still prevail). Reciting the medieval torture would imprint wise and serious concern on one's mind. It should be mentioned that John J. Robinson in his *Born in Blood: The Lost Secrets of Freemasonry* has another explanation for the penalties. He believes these were developed by the persecuted Knights Templar (not the same as the present day Templars) as protection against spies of the king and pope because the Knights were outlawed by church and state. However (and more about this later) it was the seventeenth century before penalties are mentioned. Today, and as far as can be determined, the only penalties suffered by Freemasons are expulsion from the fraternity, suspension, or reprimand.

27. The "Great Plague" of 1348 had an effect on masonry. How?

It wasn't only masons that were harmed, it was all classes that had survived the "Black Death" that had reportedly entered Great Britain (and actually the world) from Asia. It was believed that one-half, or more, of the people of England died. The laboring class is said to have taken advantage of this situation and demanded vast increases in wages. The farmers and the industrialists were drained. This brought the Parliament into the act and it adopted the Statute of Laborers in 1350. This set the wages for all workmen, including "freestone masons." History states there were numerous violations of the Statute.

28. What effect did the "Great Fire of London" have on masons?

All restrictions against "intruders" and requirements for apprenticeships were discarded. Foreign masons and builders from outside London were encouraged to help rebuild the city ruined by four days of fire. They were offered all types of inducements to work toward the rebuilding of the city. The incoming workers of the building trades were to have the same privileges as the freemen of the crafts for at least seven years. An act of the Parliament in 1667 confirmed these rights. It was reported that the devastation of September 1666 caused loss or damage to approximately 13,200 houses, 89 churches and 400 streets. An historian of the London Masons' Company considered the fire as a benefit to the masons, and the Masonic Lodges multiplied. *Grand Lodge* believes that this period brought into being "the curious mixture of English and Scottish features which are found embodied in the earliest known versions of masonic ritual."

29. Sir Christopher Wren played an important role in the rebuilding after the Great Fire. Was he a Freemason?

There's no evidence to support any claim that Sir Christopher Wren ever affiliated with speculative Freemasonry. Actually, thousands of good men who were (and are) affiliated wtih the building crafts never attached themselves to Freemasonry. Many of them probably didn't know of its existence, some never learned how to petition, and this is still true today! Gould used 42 pages in volume I of his history to abolish the myth that Wren was a Freemason.

30. Why don't we know more about the early days of Freemasonry than we do?

One word gives the reason—secrecy! This peculiarity has been the greatest enemy of the Craft. It caused Masonic Lodges to keep few, if any, records. It has kept "outsiders" as well as members from learning the true purposes of the guilds, and later the fraternity. It furnished the enemies of Freemasonry with unwarranted ammunition for their lies and exaggerations of its objectives. This was particularly rampant in Great Britain until the past decade.

31. When did the attacks against Freemasonry start?

About 1637 when Masonry began to accept non-operative men into the Craft. The secrecy imposed on theCraft's adherents aroused suspicions of the general populace. In 1698 the first known attack, in print, was addressed "To All Godly People, in the Citie of London." It warned of "the Mischiefs and Evils practiced in the Sight of God by those called Freed Masons.... For this devilish Sect of Men are Meeters in secret which swear against all without their Following." Because they meet in secret "are these not the ways of Evil-doers?" The leaflet was never reprinted. This was the forerunner of the premise of the detractors of Freemasonry to the present day.

32. When did religious zealots first attack Masonry?

Evidently it began in 1652 when objections to the Reverend James Ainslie were made to the Presbytery of Kelso because he was a Freemason. The decision, after consultation, is illuminating: "... to their judgment there is neither sinne nor scandale in that word [the Mason word] because in the purest tymes of this kirke, maisons haveing that word have been misisters; that maisons and men haveing that word have been and are daylie in our sessions, and many professors haveing that word are daylie admitted to the ordinancies." (See *Grand Lodge.*) This brief statement speaks volumes! It proves beyond a doubt that Freemasonry was known, and for the most part accepted, by good men long before Lodge records were to be found.

33. From whence comes the story of Freemasons and the Temple of Solomon?

The *Gothic Constitutions* speak of the early days of Masonry insofar as the scribes believe it to be. *Grand Lodge* manuscript, the third oldest known *Gothic* is dated A.D. 1583 and evidently copied from two other documents, says: "Euclid undertook to teach the young men Geometry, whereby they could earn their living and live honestly by building churches, temples, castles, towers, and manors. Euclid gave them charges to be true to the kind, to the lords they served, and to each other, and to call one another fellow or brother, and many other charges. King David began the Temple at Jerusalem and paid the Masons well and gave them charges. His son, Solomon, finished the Temple and sent for Masons in divers countries so that he had 24,000 workmen in stone, 3000 of whom were Masters. King Iram loved King Solomon and sent him timber. He had a son called Aymon who was master of Geometry and chief Master Mason and Master of all graving and carving as stated in the Bible. Solomon confirmed the charges of King Solomon.

34. From whence comes the ritual of Freemasonry?

A goodly portion of the ritual practiced even today by Freemasons throughout the world is also derived from the *Gothic Constitutions*. The same one mentioned above includes (abbreviated): You shall be true men of God; You shall be true to the king (country), without treason or falsehood; You shall be true to one another; You shall keep the counsel of your fellows; You shall call your brothers no foul names; You shall not take your fellow's wife, daughter or servant in villany; No Master or fellow shall supplant any other of their work. There is much more that will be familiar to all Freemasons of today.

35. Did the *Gothic Constitutions* play a role in the development of the Grand Lodge system?

Their importance in the evolution of Freemasonry in the Grand Lodge era will become evident in the sections that follow. There is no way a Freemason can ignore the teachings of their predecessors in this oldest and largest fraternity the world has ever known.

2. The Grand Lodge Era Begins

Much might be said of the noble art,
A craft that is worth esteeming in each part;
Sundry nations' nobles, and their kings also,
Oh how they sought its worth to know,
Nimrod and Solomon the wisest of all men,
Reason saw to love this science, then
I'll say no more, lest by my shallow verses I
Endeavoring to praise, should blemish Masonrie.
York, No.2 (MS) 1704
Masonic Sketches, W. J.Hughan, 1872

The above preamble first appeared a century earlier, slightly different, in *York, No. 1* (MS). It is more than what it seems to be. In case you don't decipher it, wait until you reach the end of the chapter.

36. What English Lodge records are the earliest known to exist?

Alnwick Lodge records for 1701 were found. Those for York Lodge for 1705 were also found, but after being examined and reported they were lost, as were those prior to 1712.

37. The name of Elias Ashmole comes up again in 1682. This was in connection with what?

Ashmole again mentioned Freemasonry in another diary entry for March 10, 1682: "About 5 P.M. I recd: A Summons to appr at a Lodge to be held the next day, at Masons Hall London. 11. Accordingly I went, & about Noone were admitted into the Fellowship of Freemasons.... I was the Senior Fellow among them (it being 35 years since I was admitted)." This confirms the earlier entry of 1646. He concluded: "We dyned at the halfe Moone Taverne in Cheapside, as a noble dinner prepaired at the charge of the new-accepted Masons."

38. Ashmole's diary entry confirms what often occurred after initiations. What was it?

This confirms that often newly initiated Freemasons paid for banquets for members of the Lodge. It also confirms that taverns were often utilized for Masonic functions.

39. What other evidence is there that confirms Freemasonry was active in England prior to the formation of a Grand Lodge?

Randle Holme, an author, praised the Craft in his *Academie of Armory* of 1688: "I cannot but Honor the Fellowship of the Masons because of its Antiquity, and the more as being a Member of that Society." Among his papers was found a leaflet printed in London in 1698 attacking Freemasons as "devilish"; "anti-Christ"; "corrupt."
Alnwick Lodge in the north of England published: "Orders to be observed by the Company and Fellowship of Freemasons att a Lodge held at Alnwick Septr. 29, 1701, being the Genll Head Meeting Day." This Lodge remained an operative Lodge until it went out of existence about 1763. It also remained independent, never joining any Grand Lodge.

40. Is there any validity to the statement that York has always been the center of Masonic activity?

A tough question to answer accurately. There's no evidence to support the tales that annual meetings of Freemasons were held there. The two earliest *Gothics, Regius* and *Cooke* don't mention York, but *Grand Lodge (MS)* of 1583 and *Antiquity* of 1686 say that York was where the first Assembly was held. The fabric rolls of York Minster issued in 1355 required that the "ancient customs to be faithfully observed." Then James Anderson in his *Constitutions* of 1723 (which see later) mentions York prominently. York Lodge was active at least in 1705, but it evidently became dormant in 1730. Six copies of the *Gothic Constitutions* were found in the archives of the Lodge, which would indicate that it was something of a leader in the Craft. It's interesting to note that a "York Chalice" was designed by the General Grand Chapter of Royal Arch Masons, International. In 1972 the

General Grand High Priest, Gordon Merrick, traveled to York and presented one of the first copies of this chalice to the Marquis of Zetland. (See *The Saga of the Holy Royal Arch of Freemasonry*, an international award-winning documentary film.)

41. What brought about the formation of the first Grand Lodge?

Grand Lodge probably gives as good an answer as anyone can: "... the seeds were sown in 1356 with the first code of mason regulations promulgated at Guildhall in London. Between those two dates [1356-1717] the Craft had undergone such vast industrial, economic, and social changes as to suggest that the events of 1717 were the beginning of a new and separate story."

42. What occurred during the first meeting to form a Grand Lodge?

No one knows! The first written account was found in the revision of the *Constitutions* in 1738 by Dr. James Anderson.

43. What does James Anderson tell us about the formation of the Grand Lodge of England?

Anderson writes: "... after the Rebellion [the Jacobite uprising] was over A.D. 1716, the few *Lodges at London* finding themselves neglected by Sir Christopher Wren [remember, Wren wasn't a member of the Craft], thought to cement together under a *Grand Master* as the Center of Union and Harmony, viz, the *Lodges* that met,
"1. At the *Goose and Gridiron* Ale-house in St. *Paul's Church-yard.*
"2. At the *Crown Ale-House* in *Parker's-Lane near Drury-Lane.*
"3. At the *Apple-Tree Tavern* in *Charles-street, Covent-Garden.*
"4. At the *Rummer* and *Grapes Tavern* in *Channel-Row, Westminster.*"
They met at the Apple-Tree Tavern, placed the oldest Master Mason in the chair and constituted themselves a temporary Grand Lodge. They decided to "revive" the Quarterly Communications, hold an Annual Assembly and Feast, and chose a Grand Master. No date for this meeting is mentioned.

44. When and where was the first annual communication that chose a Grand Master held?

According to Anderson: "On St. John Baptist's Day, [June 24] in the 3d Year of King George I, A.D. 1717 the ASSEMBLY and *Feast of the Free and Accepted Masons* was held at the foresaid *Goose* and *Gridiron* Ale-house."

45. Who was elected Grand Master of Masons of this first Grand Lodge?

Antony Sayer, Gentleman, a member of the Lodge meeting in the Apple-Tree Tavern. (The index of *Grand Lodge* spells his name as Anthony Sayer, but it's Antony in the early accounts.)

46. Why was it believed necessary to form a Grand Lodge?

No one knows. Anderson said it was because the Lodges felt Wren was neglecting them, but this has been discounted. *Grand Lodge* says it "appears to have been conceived purely as a gathering of London Lodges, without aspirations for power or the extending of its jurisdiction." And, actually, it was viewed as merely a local body.

47. Was a ritual followed during the meetings of the Grand Lodge?

It is doubtful that any form of ritual was known, or practiced. It appears that the meetings were held for the purpose previously stated—for fellowship and feasting.

48. Who was elected the second Grand Master?

George Payne, a government official. This occurred during the second annual meeting, June 24, 1718, at the Goose and Gridiron. He was replaced in 1719, then elected again in 1720.

49. Who was elected the third Grand Master?

Dr. John Theophilus Desaguliers, a Fellow of the Royal Society. Although he was replaced by Payne in 1720 he remained an active participant in the Grand Lodge until his death in 1744.

50. Who was the first nobleman elected Grand Master?

John, 2nd Duke of Montague (1688-1749), was elected on the recommendation of George Payne to be his successor. He was installed on June 24, 1721. From this date forward a member of the nobility, or a prince of royal blood, would head Freemasonry in England. Gould said this act of 1721 brought the Craft into public notice and esteem.

51. When was the first written account of laws for the government of the Grand Lodge published?

In 1723. Among the first acts of the new Grand Master in 1721 was to order James Anderson to digest the old *Gothic Constitutions* into a new and better method for the government of the Craft. About two years later the Grand Lodge approved the work.

52. The next two years were historically significant. What happened?

The Duke of Wharton was elected Grand Master in 1722; Francis, Earl of Dalkeith, succeeded him in 1723. Most important, William Cowper, Clerk of the Parliaments, was appointed Secretary of the Grand Lodge. From this date onward the minutes of this body were constant. *Grand Lodge* also states that the Duke of Wharton was frustrated in his attempts to control the Grand Lodge unconstitutionally so he left the hall in a huff never to return.

53. For over a century American Grand Lodges have said they have "exclusive jurisdiction" over all of Freemasonry in their jurisdictions, claiming this power was enacted by the first Grand Lodge. Is this true?

It's false. The Grand Lodge of England during its Annual Meeting of November 25, 1723 stated that "no new Lodge in or near London without it be regularly Constituted be Countenanced by the Grand Lodge, nor the Master or Wardens admitted at the Grand Lodge." Note: Only London—not England—was considered the jurisdiction of the Grand Lodge.

54. Wasn't there another Grand Lodge in England about the time of the formation noted above?

Perhaps. How long a Lodge at York, whose records start in 1712, had been in existence is unknown. The Master of the Lodge was called "President," but it evidently took note of what had transpired in 1717. In 1725 it met in what it called "The Grand Feast" and the "President" became "Grand Master." A Deputy Grand Master and Grand Wardens were also elected. The following year Francis Drake, the Junior Grand Warden, disputed the "superiority" of the Lodges in London. He added: "[W]e are content they enjoy the Title of Grand Master of *England*; but the *Totius Angliae* (of All England) we claim as an undoubted right." In other words it called itself "The Grand Lodge of All England." Within his address Drake mentioned "E.P., F.C. and M.M." (the first known mention of **three** degrees), making it probable that this Lodge was already working in three degrees! It didn't appear to do much crusading for it was 1781 before this York Grand Lodge warranted another Lodge. It went out of existence about 1792. During its existence (or dormancy) the "Modern" Grand Lodge warranted York Lodge No. 236, which in 1777 became Union Lodge. (Also see The Grand Lodge of England South of the River Trent.)

55. The "Modern" Grand Lodge? Why that term? Were there other Grand Lodges in England?

Yes. In July 1751 **The Most Antient and Honourable Society of Free and Accepted Masons according to the Old Institutions** was founded in London. It became known as the "Antients (often spelled *Ancients*) Grand Lodge" and dubbed the older Grand Lodge "the moderns."

56. Why was the "Antients" Grand Lodge founded?

The founders claimed the Grand Lodge of 1717 had drastically deviated from the customs and ritual of ancient Freemasonry. This claim had much truth to it. The critics of the Craft (they've been around since Freemasonry became known) frightened the hierarchy of the 1717 Grand Lodge. In an attempt to keep impostors out, words were changed from one degree to another, and other alterations were made. The committee that brought into being the 1751 Grand Lodge claimed the Craft had been opened to non-Christians; the Sts. John Days had been ignored (no Grand Master had been installed on those days from 1730 to 1753); the modes of recognition had been transposed; the ceremony of installing the Master of Lodges had been altered; the catechisms of each degree had been neglected. It is claimed, and it appears to be correct, that the leadership of the Grand Lodge had been weak for several years. Many eighteenth century Freemasons couldn't accept this "heresy." It is believed a group began work on the formation of this rival body as early as 1739.

57. It has been claimed that the Antients Grand Lodge was formed by Master Masons from the Moderns. Is this true?

No. The founders of the Antients were not "seceders," so there was no "schism." Not one of the first dissidents was a member of a lodge under the jurisdiction of the Moderns. They were members of Scottish and Irish Lodges.

58. Wasn't there an English Grand Lodge formed by defectors of the Moderns?

There certainly was, but it was a few years later. And it involved one of the best known English Freemasons—William Preston. He was Master of the Lodge of Antiquity, the first of the Four Old Lodges. Preston was appointed to prepare a new "Book of Constitutions." When it was nearly completed, Preston was fired and the job was given to the Treasurer of his Lodge! The Treasurer later accused Preston of holding a parade in Masonic dress, a violation of the Grand Lodge regulations. Preston claimed his Lodge, because of its antiquity, had privileges other Lodges didn't. The Lodge expelled the Treasurer and two of his cohorts! Grand Lodge demanded their reinstatement. So Preston and his followers gained permission from the York Grand Lodge to form the Grand Lodge of England South of the River Trent. They moved the furniture of the Lodge under the cover of darkness to new quarters. This new Grand Lodge existed for ten years, from 1779 to 1789, then came to a painless end when Preston and his followers were reunited with the Moderns Grand Lodge, and the Lodge of Antiquity was united again.

59. Who were the "Atholl Masons"?

This was another name given to the members of the Antients Grand Lodge. For many years the Grand Master was the Duke of Atholl.

60. How important was *The Constitutions of the Free-Masons* compiled by James Anderson and adopted in 1723?

It's the most important document in Freemasonry. Its charges and regulations are the basis for the government of all regular Masonry. Any serious deviation from them would make the Craft something other than Freemasonry.

61. What are the main points in the Charges brought out in the Constitutions of 1723?

A facsimile of the *Constitutions* can be found in several books including *Little Masonic Library*, volume 1. A digest of the points covered will be found in Key to Freemasonry's Growth. This tells us the first 48 pages were devoted to the history of Freemasonry as Anderson found it in searching the *Old Gothic Constitutions*. Eight pages contained "The Charges of a Free-Mason"; 13 pages listed 39 "General Regulations" as compiled by George Payne who was Grand Master in 1720. Abbreviated, the Charges are:

I. A Mason must be moral; must not be an atheist; must believe in God, but be tolerant of all religions.

II. A Mason must obey the civil laws; must be patriotic.

III. Every Mason ought to belong to a lodge; a member must be good and true, freeborn, male, and of legal age.

IV. Officers must be chosen by merit, not by seniority or favoritism; apprentices must be perfect in body and capable of learning the art and being of service; work must be learned before becoming a Warden; a Master must have served as a Warden; a Grand Master must have served as a Master and he can choose a Past Master as his Deputy.

V. Masons must perform honest work; Master must pay just wages; envy of a Brother is forbidden; supplanting a Brother in his work is not allowed; Wardens shall be true to the Master and Brothers must obey them; young Brothers shall be instructed to continue practicing Brotherly Love; Grand Lodge must approve working tools; Masons shall not teach unaccepted masons.

VI. 1. Behavior in lodge must be exemplary; a complaint against a Brother is to be judged by the lodge, and may be appealed to the Grand Lodge; no lawsuit against Masonry is to be instituted without the consent of the lodge.

2. Without the lodge, all excesses must be avoided; no private piques or quarrels are to be brought into a lodge, nor is a discussion of religion or politics admissible.

3. Brothers are to greet each other in a courteous manner and they are to meet upon the level.

4. Masons are to be cautious in their words and carriage.

5. Masons must be moral and faithful husbands; they must keep the happenings of the lodge from the outside world; they must not be gluttons or drunkards.

6. Genuine Brothers must be aided, if in want.

62. How did Anderson end his list of Charges?

He closed this section by writing:
"Finally, All these Charges you are to observe, and also those that shall be communicated to you in another way; cultivating BROTHERLY-LOVE, the Foundation and Cape-stone, the Cement and Glory of this ancient Fraternity, avoiding all Wrangling and Quarreling, all slander and Backbiting, not permitting others to slander any honest Brother, but defending his Character, and doing him all good Offices, as far as is consistent with your Honour and Safety, and no further. And if any of them do you Injury, you must apply to your own or his Lodge; and from thence you may appeal to the GRAND LODGE at the Quarterly Communication, and from thence to the annual GRAND LODGE, as has been the ancient laudable conduct of our Fore-fathers in every Nation; never taking a legal course but when the Case cannot be otherwise decided, and patiently listening to the honest and friendly Advice of Master and Fellows, when they would prevent your going to Law with Strangers, or would excite you to put a speedy Period to all Law-Suits, that so you may mind the Affair of Masonry with the more Alacrity and Success; but with respect to Brothers or Fellows at Law, the Master and Brethren should kindly offer their Mediation, which ought to be thankfully submitted to by the contending Brethren; and if that Submission is impracticable, they must however carry on their Process, or Law-Suits, without Wrath and Rancor (not in the common way) saying or doing nothing which may hinder Brotherly Love, and good Offices to be renew'd and continu'd that all may see the benign Influence of MASONRY, as all true Masons have done from the Beginning of the World, and will do to the End of Time. Amen. So Mote It Be."

63. What were the General Regulations?

Again Payne's 39 General Regulations were abbreviated in *Key*. It's interesting to note how closely most Grand Lodges follow these to this day:
1. The Grand Master, or his Deputy, has the authority to preside over any lodge he visits.
2. The Master has the right to congregate his members into a lodge at his pleasure; in his absence, one of his Wardens may do so.
3. Minutes and by-laws must be kept.
4. No more than five Brethren shall receive degrees at one time; 25 shall be the minimum age.

5. One month shall elapse between receiving a petition and election.
6. A unanimous ballot is necessary to elect a petitioner.
7. Every new Brother shall contribute to charity in addition to paying the amount stated in the by-laws.
8. No group of members shall withdraw from the lodge except to form a new one, and even then a dispensation must be obtained from the Grand Master or his Deputy.
9. An unruly Brother shall be twice admonished and then suffer such penalty as is stated in the by-laws.
10. The Master and Wardens, being representatives of the lodge at Grand Lodge, shall receive instructions from the members.
11. The same ritual shall be practiced, insofar as possible in each lodge.
12. The Grand Lodge shall consist of the Masters and Wardens of the lodges, as well as Grand Lodge officers, quarterly communications shall be held.
13. At the Annual Communication, business shall be consummated; differences must be reconciled; annual reports of lodges filed; means of dispensing charity decided.
14. If the Grand Master and his Deputy are absent, "The present Master of a lodge that has been the longest a Free-Mason" shall preside.
15. The Grand Master shall appoint Wardens, *pro tempore*, if the Grand Wardens are absent.
16. All lodges shall reach the Grand Master only through his Deputy.
17. The Grand Master, Grand Wardens, Grand Treasurer, and Grand Secretary cannot be Master or Wardens of a lodge.
18. The Grand Master must receive the concurrence of Grand Lodge to replace his Deputy.
19. As all Past Grand Masters have "behaved themselves," a new regulation will have to be adopted should one act unworthily.
20. The Grand Master, his Deputy and Wardens, shall visit every lodge in town at least once during his term.
21. In case of the death of the Grand Master, the office shall revert to the junior Past Grand Master.
22. A new Grand Master must be chosen every year on St. John's Day.
23. If it is decided to hold a Grand Feast, "according to the ancient laudable Custom of Masons," the Grand Wardens shall handle the arrangements, but a committee of Steward may be appointed to assist them.
24. The Grand Master may call a meeting of the Masters and Wardens for any emergency.

The Grand Lodge Era Begins 23

25. The Master of each lodge shall appoint a Fellowcraft to make certain that all admitted to the Feast are true Brothers.
26. The Grand Master shall appoint two or more Doorkeepers.
27. The grand Wardens, or Stewards, shall appoint a number of *free and accepted Masons* to serve at the tables.
28. All the Members of Grand Lodge must be at the place of meeting long before dinner in order:
   1. To receive any appeals.
   2. To prevent differences that might destroy the Harmony and Pleasure of the Grand Feast.
   3. To prevent all indecency and ill Manners.
   4. To receive and consider motions.
29. After the foregoing, the Grand officers shall retire to let the Masters and Wardens of the lodges determine who shall be the Grand Master for the next year.
30. The Brethren may converse freely until seated at the Table.
31. After dinner, the Grand Lodge is opened.
32. "If the Grand Master of last year has consented" to continue in office, he shall be requested "to do the FRATERNITY *the great honour* (if nobly born, if not *the great kindness)* of continuing to be their *Grand Master* for the Year ensuing."
33. If not elected, or not agreeing to serve, the Grand Master shall nominate his successor, and if he is unanimously elected, he shall be proclaimed, saluted and congratulated.
34. If not unanimously approved, the new Grand Master shall be chosen by ballot; every Master and Warden shall write his man's name; the last Grand Master shall write his man's name, and the man whose name is drawn by the last Grand Master shall become the Grand Master for the ensuing year.
35. The Grand Master shall appoint his Deputy; the Grand Wardens shall be nominated by the Grand Master, and if not elected unanimously they are to be chosen by ballot in the same manner as the Grand Master; the same rule applies to the Wardens of the lodges.
36. If the new Grand Master is not present, he cannot be proclaimed unless someone can vouch that he will accept, in which case the old Grand Master shall do the appointing and nominating in the name of the new Grand Master.
37. The Grand Master shall allow any "Brother, Fellowcraft, or Apprentice to speak, directing his Discourse to his Worship."
38. The Brethren then shall be given some good advice, and the Grand Lodge closed in a form "that cannot be written in any language."
39. Every Grand Lodge "has an inherent Power and Authority to make

new Regulations, or to alter these, for the real Benefit of this ancient Fraternity, provided always that the old LAND-MARKS be carefully preserv'd."

64. What are Freemasonry's Landmarks?

To be safe, they are what one's Grand Lodge says they are! To be truthful, no one can honestly enumerate them! Even Albert Mackey claimed: "... the unwritten laws or customs of Masonry constitute its Landmarks, and that the written law is to be obtained in the regulations made by the supreme Masonic authority, and which are either general or local, as the authority which enacted them was either general or local in its character." In short, a Landmark is something that can't be written. And that's as honestly as anyone can state the case. BUT, then Mackey goes on to list 25!! Strangely, 13 American Grand Lodges adopted his list, eight use them by custom, 20 have adopted none (correctly), 10 have developed their own. Masonic scholars tore Mackey's reasoning apart.

65. What did Robert Freke Gould, the great English historian, say about landmarks?

He said he had searched in vain for a list of Landmarks. He came to the conclusion: "Nobody knows that they comprise or omit; they are of no earthly authority, because everything is a landmark when an opponent desires to silence you; but nothing is a landmark that stands in his own way." That's about as accurate as one can get on this subject.

66. When was the Grand Lodge of Ireland formed? And the Grand Lodge of Scotland?

Between 1725 and 1730, but it appears the exact date cannot be determined for the formation of the Grand Lodge of Ireland. Without question, the Grand Lodge of Scotland was established in 1736.

67. Who was Laurence Dermott?

Dermott was considered by many to be the most remarkable Freemason who ever lived. The Antients Grand Lodge which was formed in 1751 appointed him its Grand Secretary. As such he kept his Grand Lodge in the forefront of Freemasonry until 1787, four years before his death. He was the author of *Ahiman Rezon*, the book of Constitutions for the Antients. The original contained nothing derogatory to the Moderns, but later editions strongly condemned the earlier Grand Lodge. Dermott was a staunch advocate of the Royal Arch, considering it "the root, heart and marrow of Masonry."

68. Who was the most active "Modern" Mason at the time Dermott was active with the Antients?

Thomas Dunckerley, and his life, especially his work for Freemasonry, is well worth studying. He served in the Royal Navy (after running away to sea before he reached 11 years of age!) for 26 years. In 1754 he was made a Mason in the Lodge at the Three Tuns at Portsmouth in 1754, and during the same year he was made a Royal Arch Mason. He was given a traveling warrant in 1760 for a lodge to be held aboard *H.M.S. Vanguard*. Two years later he received another warrant for a Lodge aboard the *Prince*. He later used these warrants to form Lodges in London. He later was appointed to several Provincial Grand Masterships at a time when this position (and those appointed to it) was virtually dormant. In the Royal Arch, Dunckerley had wider authority and was able to make it an integral part of Freemasonry.

69. What does *Ahiman Rezon* mean?

A question many have endeavored to interpret with but limited success. It has been termed "A Help to a Brother"; "Faithful Brother Secretary"; "Will of Selected Brethren"; "Law of Prepared Brethren"; "Secrets of a Prepared Brother"; "Royal Builder"; "The Thoughts or Opinions of a True and Faithful Brother." Take your pick! And a little research will reveal other translations. For certain, it was the Book of Constitutions for the Antients Grand Lodge.

70. Did the two main rival Grand Lodges ever agree on anything?

During the latter part of the eighteenth century many leading Freemasons participated in the work of both. In fact, in 1809 the Modern Grand Lodge, by resolution, admitted it had deviated from the ancient landmarks beginning in about 1739. This helped pave the way for a joining of the rivals.

71. Did James Anderson update his Constitutions of 1723?

He did. In 1738 his *New Book of Constitutions* was published. Within its pages the first account of the formation of the Grand Lodge (Moderns) is recorded. Here he says soon after the formation older Brethren who had ignored the call to form a Grand Lodge began visiting and taking an interest in the revival of speculative Freemasonry. He said that in 1721 John Duke of Montagu was saluted as Grand Master Elect. And arrangements were made to move the next meeting of the Grand Lodge from a tavern to Stationers' Hall. This was considered a step upward. A public procession of Masons began and would continue until 1747, when anti-Masons caused the leaders of the Craft to abandon visible appearances. The 1738 *Constitutions* is interesting, and historical, reading.

72. Did the Moderns Grand Lodge grow in strength?

No. In 1770 the Grand Lodge had 160 Lodges in London; in 1800, 100; 1813, 85. In the Provinces, where the rivalry between the Antients and Moderns was less pronounced, both Grand Lodges were holding their own.

73. When did the leadership begin considering a union of the two Grand Lodges?

It's difficult to say, but in 1806 the Earl of Moira visited the Grand Lodge of Scotland and was told there should be a consolidation. He said the Antients had rejected overtures for a union. But in February 1809 the Moderns passed a resolution ordering its Lodges to revert to the Ancient Landmarks of the Society from which it had deviated about 1739. In October of the same year it established a "Lodge of Masons for the purpose of ascertaining and promulgating the Ancient Land Marks of the Society and instructing the Craft in all such matters..."

74. What were the acts of fate that brought about the Union of the rival Grand Lodges in 1813?

The Earl of Moira, Grand Master of the Moderns, had met early in 1811 with the Duke of Atholl, Grand Master of the Antients to discuss a union. Early in 1813 the former was appointed Governor-General of Bengal and the Duke of Sussex became Grand Master of the Moderns. The Duke of Atholl, now living in Scotland, recommended that the Duke of Kent be elected Grand Master in his stead. This brought Royal brothers into the two Grand Masterships. They favored a union. Consequently Articles of Union were signed on November 25, 1813. A united Grand Assembly was scheduled for Freemasons' Hall for December 27, 1813.

To return to the beginning: Did you decipher the hidden key in the preamble? Circle, underline, or highlight the first letter in each line. You will then find the last word in the jingle—MASONRIE.

3. Freemasonry in Early North America

It is now Thirty Seven years since I was admitted into the Ancient and Hon'ble Society of Free and accepted Masons, to whom I have been a faithful Brother, & well-wisher to the Art of Masonry.

I shall ever maintain a strict friendship for the whole Fraternity; and always be glad when it may fall in my power to do them any service.

-Jonathan Belcher, *Royal Governor in Massachusetts,* September 25, 1741-

75. When did Freemasonry start in North America? Who were the first known Freemasons in the Colonies of North America?

As with the beginning of Freemasonry, no one knows when the Craft came to the shores of North America. In October 1682 John Skene, a member of Aberdeen Lodge No. 1 in Scotland, settled in Burlington, New Jersey. He became deputy governor in 1685. Jonathan Belcher was probably made a Mason in England in 1704, and later became Royal Governor of Massachusetts. He was an affiliate of St. John's Lodge in Boston. (See quote at the beginning of this chapter.)

76. Didn't the first sign of Freemasonry in North America appear in Nova Scotia?

Perhaps. A stone engraved on the top with a square and compasses was found on the shore of Goat Island in the Annapolis Basin in Nova Scotia. In the center of the flat slab was the date 1606. Dr. Charles T. Jackson of Boston wrote about it in 1829, calling it the "Annapolis Stone." McLeod writes: "No doubt it was the grave marker for a French stonemason who had settled at Port Royal with DeMonts and Champlain in 1605." This stone is said to have become a part of a wall for a building; it was covered with cement and never found again.

77. Did Benjamin Franklin mention Freemasonry before he became a member of the Craft?

He did. In the pages of his *Pennsylvania Gazette* for December 5-8, 1730 was this item: "As there are several Lodge of Free-Masons erected in the Province, and People have lately been much amus'd with Conjectures concerning them; we think the following Account of Free-Masonry from London, will not be unacceptable to our Readers." It then mentioned the death of a fellow who had a satirical article in his possession.

78. Who was appointed by the Grand Lodge of England as first Provincial Grand Master in North America?

From a report of the Board of General Purposes of the United Grand Lodge of England in 1930 confirms that on June 1, 1730 the Grand Master (Duke of Norfolk) signed a warrant naming Daniel Coxe the first Provincial Grand Master of North America. According to the statement Coxe's domain included Massachusetts, Pennsylvania, New Jersey and New York.

79. When did the first Masonic Lodge meeting take place in North America?

The first record of a Lodge meeting is found in "Liber B," an account book of St. John's Lodge in Philadelphia. ("Liber A," unfortunately, has never been located.) It begins with entries on June 24, 1731; ends on June 24, 1738. It showed that the Lodge had met earlier, but when is unknown. It showed William Allen was "Grand Master" of a Grand Lodge that had been formed according to the custom then prevailing.

80. When did Benjamin Franklin became a Freemason?

In February 1731.

81. When did Franklin become a Grand Master?

On June 24, 1734.

82. When did Freemasonry begin in Massachusetts?

No one knows. (Perhaps it should be mentioned here that there has always been a dearth of records concerning Freemasonry. This could well be because of the unwarranted belief in the need for secrecy, but it could also be because of laziness which exists even today.) When the first Lodge was formed in 1733 at least ten of the members had been made Masons in Boston earlier. Where or when isn't known.

83. Who was Henry Price?

Henry Price, according to Melvin M. Johnson, was appointed in April 1733 Provincial Grand Master of New England and Dominions and Territories thereunto belonging. On July 30, 1733 he formed a Grand Lodge in Boston. There is some question about this appointment, but as will become evident later, Henry Price was an excellent servant to the Craft throughout his life.

84. Did Henry Price and Benjamin Franklin ever meet?

Josiah Hayden Drummond of Maine (about whom more later) said in Gould's history that they met in Boston, Massachusetts, in the autumn of 1733, but a letter written in 1734 by Franklin to Price proved that they were strangers.

85. Why did Franklin write to Price?

As with far too many things, this is open to differing interpretations. It would appear that Franklin wanted to find out for sure who was the Masonic authority in America. He, Franklin, was Grand Master in Pennsylvania and he read in the press that Price's "power extended over all America." Price never answered Franklin's letter.

86. How many times did Price serve as Provincial Grand Master?

Four times: 1733-1737; 1740-1744; 1754-1755; 1767-1768. He was also the first Master of Master's Lodge and the Second Lodge in Boston. He also served as Master of the First Lodge.

87. When and how did Henry Price die?

At the age of 83 he was fatally injured while splitting logs. On May 14, 1780 his ax slipped and struck him in his abdomen. He died on the 20th.

88. When did Freemasonry make an appearance in Georgia?

Grand Lodge records that Roger Lacy was appointed Provincial Grand Master for Georgia in 1735. It also says he was an affiliated member of the Lodge at Savannah (later Solomon's Lodge No. 1) "of which [James Edward] Oglethorpe was the first Master in 1734."

89. When was the Grand Lodge of Georgia formed?

On December 16, 1786, although it dates its birth from December 2, 1735 when Roger Lacy was appointed P.G.M.

90. What part did the Grand Lodge of England play in the establishment of Georgia as a colony?

In 1733 the Grand Lodge of England agreed to ask its members and Lodges to assist those who had been appointed "to send distressed Brethren to Georgia where they may be comfortably provided for."

91. Who were the "distressed Brethren" referred to by the Grand Lodge of England?

Oglethorpe had long been interested in helping those confined to prison because they were unable to pay their bills. One of his solutions was to take these men to the new world where they would be free to form a new life. The king and politicians agreed to the formation of a colony that would act as a buffer against the advancement of the Spaniards into the colonies to the east. The territory to be called "Georgia" was considered ideal. And this proved true in 1742 when the Georgians whipped the Spaniards in the Battle of Bloody Marsh.

92. Where is the first evidence of Freemasonry in South Carolina found?

On October 29, 1736 the *South Carolina Gazette* reported a meeting of a Masonic Lodge in Charleston. *Grand Lodge* recorded a warrant had been granted for Solomon's Lodge "the previous year" and it had been listed as number 251. But it was 1760 before it appeared on the English lists! For more than a decade nothing was heard (or known) about this Lodge except what is recorded in the press.

93. What did the *Gazette* report in 1740 about the Freemasons of South Carolina?

"The Ancient and Honorable Society of Free and Accepted Masons contributed the sum of two hundred and fifty pounds" to the relief of victims of a fire. Every house for more than a block had been destroyed by fire. The sum donated amounted to about $25 per Mason.

94. Shortly after the above account not much was reported about Freemasonry in the press. Why?

In 1741 the Grand Lodge of England issued a decree forbidding the publication of any part of the proceedings of a Lodge! This order was probably an outgrowth of the increase of "Mock Masonry" for more than a decade in England. Up to this time the *Gazette* carried several items, and comprises the only record of early Freemasonry in South Carolina.

95. Why was a "Masters' Lodge" formed in 1756?

A majority of creditable Masonic historians believe most, if not all, Lodges in the early years conferred only two degrees. The degree of Master Mason was conferred in a Masters' Lodge. It is pointed out that this was done in Philadelphia and Boston earlier and probably found its way to Charleston, South Carolina.

96. Did the establishment of an Antients Grand Lodge in England influence the Craft in South Carolina?

Indeed it did. There are those who believe the antagonism between the Moderns and Antients in South Carolina was more bitter than in any other jurisdiction. Barnard Elliott was elected Grand Master of the "Moderns" in 1777, and Albert Mackey claimed this formed the first independent Grand Lodge in the new United States. But many of the Loyalist Masons ignored this Grand Lodge. They elected a Provincial Grand Master in 1781. Five antient Lodges met in convention on January 1, 1787 and voted to form a Grand Lodge. On February 5 they met and elected officers; they were installed on March 24, 1787.

97. When was a single Grand Lodge formed in South Carolina?

After a series of meetings between representatives of the rival Grand Lodges beginning in 1807. But it wasn't until December 27, 1817 that the Grand Lodge of Ancient Freemasons (AFM) of South Carolina came into being with the installation of its officers.

98. Were there "Time Immemorial" Masonic Lodges in North Carolina?

Without question there were Time Immemorial Lodges in all of the original colonies in the New World. Records concerning them are scarce -- meaning, usually non-existent. When Freemasons got together they met as *Freemasons*, regularly ignoring Grand Lodges, even if they knew about them. At least two of these Lodges have been reported to have existed in North Carolina, but the first recorded Lodge was formed in Wilmington in 1754. It became St. John's and received the number 213 from the Grand Lodge of England.

99. Who was Cornelius Harnett?

He was the Master of St. John's Lodge for many years. He may have been responsible for the formation of Cabin Point Royal Arch Lodge in Virginia. He was president of the Sons of Liberty and led the fight against British taxes. Until his death in 1781 he was considered one of the king's most dangerous enemies in North Carolina.

100. It has been widely reported that the oldest Masonic Temple in North America is that of Royal White Hart Lodge in Halifax, North Carolina. Is this a fact?

No. The oldest Masonic Hall (temple) still in existence and being used exclusively for Masonic purposes is Masons' Hall in Richmond, Virginia. The Richmond hall was occupied July 11, 1786; the hall in Halifax was occupied on December 15, 1821. Why the claim by the Halifax Lodge? Its early attempts to build a Lodge were probably interpreted to mean a Lodge building had actually been accomplished.

101. Who was elected the first Grand Master of Masons in North Carolina?

Samuel Johnston was elected on December 10, 1787. When North Carolina became a state, he was its first senator; in 1787 he was its governor.

102. When did Freemasonry begin in Virginia?

It becomes tiresome to write (and read) "No one knows!" But, unfortunately, when one tries to find answers about the beginnings of Freemasonry *anywhere* he encounters numerous problems. There have been (and are) many "historians" who will manufacture history to their conception, or the way they think it should be. Factually, the first Lodge to receive a warrant from any Grand Lodge was "The Royal Exchange in the Borough of Norfolk in Virginia - First Thursd. - Dec. 22 1733." This entry, published in the 1764 engraved list of Lodges as published by Cole in England, has caused no end of problems. The entry appears after a Lodge with the date of Dec. 20, 1753, and before an entry with Jan. 31, 1754. Those historians who claim the "1733" must be a misprint appear to be correct. To add credence to this statement, the official history of the United Grand Lodge of England, *Grand Lodge 1717-1967*, states that this warrant was issued 20 December 1753. This being said, it's impossible to believe that Freemasonry in a port town as large as Norfolk wasn't known prior to the reception of a warrant (charter). And there are several other places in Virginia where Freemasonry could have been extremely active. But there are no records available to say so.

103. What is the earliest recorded date that mentions Freemasonry in Virginia.

On April 5, 1751 the *Virginia Gazette* published an announcement of a gathering of "the ancient and loyall Society of free and accepted Masons" that had taken place "some time ago."

104. Didn't the Lodge at Fredericksburg make George Washington a Freemason?

This interesting Lodge held its first recorded meeting on September 1, 1752 *with a full slate of officers*. On November 4, 1752 George Washington received the first degree in Masonry. Washington became a Fellowcraft on March 3, 1753; a Master Mason, August 4, 1753. It should be noted, this Lodge was an "immemorial Lodge"; it was July 21, 1758 before the Grand Lodge of Scotland granted it a charter.

105. The first recording of the conferral of the Royal Arch Degree occurred when and where?

The Royal Arch Degree was conferred in the Lodge at Fredericksburg, Virginia, on December 22, 1753. Simon Frazier, "an instructor in the latest methods of military science and tactics," presided as Grand Master "of a Royal Arch Lodge" and three candidates were "Raised to the Degree of Royal Arch Mason."

106. There has been some talk about a Lodge warranting other Lodges. Did this occur?

It did. Fredericksburg Lodge, for instance, warranted two Lodges, one in Falmouth another in Gloucester. The one in Gloucester, Botetourt Lodge, helped form the Grand Lodge of Virginia! It is common knowledge that Kilwinning Lodge in Scotland (which for years wouldn't join the Grand Lodge there) warranted many Lodges in many places. It was asked for a charter by Port Royal Kilwinning Crosse Lodge in Virginia, but it was the Grand Lodge of Scotland that gave this Lodge a warrant on December 1, 1755.

107. Did the Provincial Grand Lodge of Massachusetts warrant a Lodge in Maryland?

The minutes of that PGL claim it did on July 13, 1750 for "the Lodge at Mary Land"; and on August 12, 1750 for Brethren in Annapolis. These were granted by Thos. Oxnard. Prior to 1764 it appears they celebrated the Festivals of the Sts. John.

108. When did the Grand Lodge of England (Moderns) issue a warrant for a Lodge in Maryland?

On August 8, 1765 Lord Blaney, Grand Master, issued a warrant for Joppa Lodge No. 346. But it appears the members of this Lodge made a mistake. They thought they had applied for a warrant from the Antient Grand Lodge! The Grand Lodge of Pennsylvania wouldn't recognize the Lodge until 1782, when it was chartered by Pennsylvania.

109. Who was elected the first Grand Master of Masons in Maryland and when?

John Coats was elected on July 31, 1783. *But* it didn't meet again for three years, then in 1787, it again went through the motions of forming a Grand Lodge.

110. Which jurisdiction warranted most early Lodges in Delaware?

Pennsylvania. This Provincial Grand Lodge warranted a Lodge at Cantwell's Bridge (between Dover and Wilmington) on June 24, 1765. It remained extremely active, becoming Union No. 5 under the Grand Lodge of Delaware. The Lodge that became Washington No. 1 was warranted by Pennsylvania at Christiana Ferry (Wilmington) as No. 14 on December 27, 1769.

111. When did the Lodges meet to form the Grand Lodge of Delaware?

Four Lodges met on June 6, 1806 and completed formation of the Grand Lodge the following day.

112. What was the first known Masonic book published in the New World?

In 1734 Benjamin Franklin published James Anderson's *Constitutions* of 1723.

113. When did an early account of Freemasonry appear in a New York newspaper?

The New York *Gazette* published a "letter to the editor" in its November 26, 1737 issue. It was an attack on the secrecy of the "FREE MASONS." They "meet with their Doors shut, and a Guard at the outside to prevent any approach near to hear what they are doing." It went on to quote an obligation as it appeared in Samuel Prichard's *Masonry Dissected* which had been published in England in 1730. A notice of a Lodge meeting was published by the same paper on

January 22, 1739. The "Grand Master" had ordered the meeting to be held "at the Montgomerie Arms Tavern."

114. When was the Lodge formed that furnished the Bible on which George Washington (and several later Presidents of the United States) took the oath of office?

The Lodge was St. John's and it was warranted in 1757.

115. What problems did the Freemasons in New York encounter in an attempt to form a Grand Lodge?

With the close of the War for American Independence (often called the "Revolution") the Antients Lodges called a convention on January 23, 1781. Representatives from seven Lodges elected the Reverend William Walter as Grand Master. This action was sanctioned by John, Duke of Atholl, Grand Master of the Antients Grand Lodge. BUT the New York body was considered a Provincial Grand Lodge! It adopted a resolution which agreed to accept "Modern" Masons once they were "healed and admitted into the mysteries of the Ancient Craft." With the war's final end, the British sympathizers left New York, along with Grand Master Walter. Robert R. Livingston, Chancellor of the State of New York, was elected Grand Master. The Antients (Atholl) Provincial Grand Lodge had come to an end. Livingston called an emergency meeting on June 2, 1784 to bring the Moderns and Antients together.

116. Did harmony prevail in New York after the new Grand Lodge was formed?

No. The country Lodges didn't like the way the Lodges were numbered, nor did they like the "city Masons" holding all but one of the offices. The Grand Lodge adopted a resolution giving all Lodges twenty days to pay their dues and swear allegiance to the Grand Lodge or be erased from the records of the Grand Lodge. That did it! The dues were paid. On September 3, 1788 the seal was changed to read "Grand Lodge of New York."

117. What happened after this "rebellion" in New York was brought under control?

The country and city Lodges continued their rivalry. Several city Lodges broke away and formed another Grand Lodge. This lasted until June 6, 1827 when the city and country Lodges united, and on the 7th they elected Stephen Van Rensselaer Grand Master. The name was again changed. This time it became "The Grand Lodge of the Most Ancient and Honorable Fraternity of Free Masons of the State of New York."

118. Did Freemasonry enter Rhode Island in 1658?

Unlikely. A scrap of paper was said to be found that was claimed the degrees of Masonry were practiced in Newport, Rhode Island, in 1658. This scrap of paper has never since been found. A long investigation in later years could find nothing to corroborate this account.

119. When was a warrant issued for the first authentic Lodge in Rhode Island?

Thomas Oxnard, Provincial Grand Master of St. John's Provincial Grand Lodge of Massachusetts, granted a warrant for St. John's Lodge of Newport, Rhode Island, on December 27, 1749. The Master, for some unexplained reason, withheld the warrant. A second warrant was issued on May 14, 1753. The Lodge was ordered to confer only two degrees, but it ignored the order. It wasn't punished, however, and a warrant for the formation of a Masters' Lodge was granted on January 18, 1757.

120. Who warranted the second Lodge in Rhode Island?

Jeremy Gridley issued a warrant for another St. John's Lodge, this one in Providence, on January 18, 1757. It was charged to celebrate the Feasts of the Sts. John annually. This Lodge, as did so many others in the 18th century, met in private homes and taverns.

121. When was the Grand Lodge with the longest name in Freemasonry organized?

The longest name for a Grand Lodge belongs to the smallest state! On June 27, 1791, on the Festival of St. John the Baptist, in the state house in Newport, Rhode Island, previously elected Grand

Lodge officers were installed. It was officially named "The Grand Lodge of the Most Ancient and Honorable Society of Free and Accepted Masons for the State of Rhode Island and Providence Plantations." The name has never been changed. Interestingly, when the first meeting of the Grand Lodge was closed its members marched to Trinity Church. A collection was taken and was ordered to be invested in wood to be distributed to the poor during the winter.

122. Organized Freemasonry was introduced in Connecticut by whom and when?

St. John's Provincial Grand Lodge of Massachusetts warranted Hiram Lodge in New Haven on August 12, 1750. It became number 143 on the roster of the Grand Lodge of England (Moderns). David Wooster, who would become an outstanding patriot, would later become the Master of this Lodge.

123. From whence did American Union Lodge receive its warrant?

On February 15, 1776 the Provincial Grand Lodge of Massachusetts chartered American Union Lodge. This Lodge met throughout the War for American Independence. It was reactivated at Marietta, Ohio, in 1790 and later became number one on the roster of the Grand Lodge of Ohio.

124. When did the Grand Lodge of Connecticut come into being?

It took two conventions, but on July 8, 1789 the Grand Lodge was "perfected."

125. Who was installed as the first Grand Master in New Hampshire? When?

John Sullivan, the "President of the State of New Hampshire," was elected on July 16, 1789; he was installed on April 8, 1790.

4. Forming a Republic

Resolved, That every member of this Congress considers himself under the ties of virtue, honour, and love of his country, not to divulge, directly or indirectly, any matter or thing agitated or debated in Congress, before the same shall have been determined, without leave of the Congress; nor any matter or thing determined in Congress, which a majority of the Congress shall order to be kept secret. And that if any member shall violate this agreement, he shall be expelled from this Congress, and deemed an enemy to the liberties of America, and liable to be treated as such; and that every member signify his consent to this agreement by signing the same.

Adopted by the Continental Congress,
November 9, 1775.

126. When and where did the First Continental Congress begin meeting?

In Philadelphia on September 5, 1774.

127. Who was the first President chosen for the First Continental Congress?

A Past Master of Williamsburg Lodge, Peyton Randolph.

128. What led to the formation of the first and other Continental Congresses?

"Taxation without representation" is said to be the principal cause of dissatisfaction with Great Britain and its politicians. Ironically, the Grand Lodges in England didn't tax their member Lodges.

They asked for no per capita fees, but did request contributions to their charitable projects.

129. Where was the oath of secrecy recorded at the beginning of this chapter found?

It is quoted from *Secret Journals of the Acts and Proceedings of U.S. Congress*, vol. 1, p. 34. It was recorded in *Documents Illustrative of the Formation of the Union of the American States*, Government Printing Office, 1927.

130. Was the vow of secrecy upheld by all the members of the Continental Congress?

Without question the vow of secrecy was kept. About 25 years passed before the first report of what occurred was revealed. The same policy was followed during the Constitutional Convention over which George Washington presided in 1787.

131. Did Freemasonry play a role in exploiting the difficulties with England?

Freemasonry has never exploited complications in any area. In fact, there is plenty of evidence to prove that Freemasonry (meaning Lodges and Grand Lodges as a whole) has always acted as a peace maker. As Freemasons have always been free to act as their consciences dictate, many would be found on both sides of the issues then prevailing. This would always prove true.

132. Were Freemasons involved in the "Boston Tea Party" that took place on December 16, 1773?

No one knows! To this day (1993) not a single "Indian" has ever been identified. There have been spurious claims made about some of the participants, and even books purporting to list names of those involved, there has never been any positive proof. St. Andrews Lodge, which met in the Green Dragon Tavern, didn't meet the evening Boston harbor was turned into a giant tea pot, because there weren't enough members present. But the lack of attendance wasn't uncommon. It has been claimed the Secretary of the Lodge ended minutes of the meeting with a large "T". This isn't true. The large mark was simply a scroll. Although it may be true (and likely) that Freemasons were among the tea tossers, there is absolutely no way to ascertain this one way or the other.

133. What was the direct cause for turning Boston harbor into a giant tea pot?

The Townshend Acts had aroused the ire of the Colonists; it was a threepenny tax on tea for the Colonies (England was tax-exempt) that caused the Bostonians to determine to not "take it any more."

134. Was the Boston Tea Party the first violence against a British ship prior to the War for American Independence?

No. The *Gaspee,* a British warship, was destroyed on June 8, 1772. Without question, Rhode Island Freemasons were among the leaders. The *Gaspee* had been blockading the coast. Its captain demanded the schooner "Hannah" submit to a search. The "Hannah" evaded the British vessel, and the *Gaspee* ran aground. Rhode Islanders surprised the British, climbed aboard, set the crew ashore and burned the vessel. This was the first combative act between the Colonists and British in what would become a long war.

135. Did the Colonies have any champions in the British Parliament?

They did. Edmund Burke, a member of Jerusalem Lodge No. 33, pleaded for conciliation with America. He wasn't successful. John Wilkes was imprisoned for writing a political pamphlet, "Thoughts on the Present Discontents," favorable toward the Colonies. Members of Burke's Lodge went to the prison and made John Wilkes a Mason on March 3, 1769.

136. What brought about Patrick Henry's "Liberty or Death" speech? Was he a Freemason?

Patrick Henry wasn't a Freemason. His famous speech was the result of Lord John Murray Dunmore, Virginia's governor, suspending the Virginia Assembly. It moved to Richmond where on March 23, 1775 it met in St. John's Church. The speech made by Henry was off-the-cuff, but later reconstructed by William Wirt.

137. Who gave the signal from the Old North Church in Boston to Paul Revere and others about the intentions of the British?

It was a Freemason, but which one is uncertain. Robert Newman was a member of St. John's Lodge; John Pulling, Jr., was a member of St. Andrew's. Paul Revere was a member of St. Andrew's.

138. Were Freemasons involved in the Battle of Bunker Hill?

Definitely. But how many on both sides will never be ascertained. It is known that the battle (really on Breed's Hill, not Bunker) was a blunder by the colonists. The hill was impossible to entrench or defend. But "the rabble in arms," so-called by the British command, shocked the English. It took three attacks, British reinforcements, and the scarcity of ammunition for the defenders to be defeated. Dr. Joseph Warren, Grand Master of the Scottish Grand Provincial Lodge, was killed, fighting as a private with the Americans rather than the general he was. This battle caused the lack-luster Continental Congress to reassess its priorities. It chose a Commander-in-Chief.

139. Who did the Second Continental Congress select as Commander-in-Chief of American forces?

George Washington, a member of the Lodge at Fredericksburg in the colony of Virginia, the logical man because of his army experience, was chosen unanimously. The deed was done on July 15, 1775.

140. What did the new Commander do?

He left for Boston immediately after his selection. There he began the task of turning the "rabble" into a fighting machine. In September he sent two forces to attack Montreal and Quebec. He placed two Freemasons in command: General Richard Montgomery (Lodge of Unity No. 18, I.C.) to Montreal; Benedict Arnold (an affiliated member of Hiram Lodge No. 1 in Connecticut since 1765) to Quebec. Montgomery managed to capture Montreal. He later joined forces with Arnold and was killed at Quebec. Arnold was wounded but kept Quebec under siege until July 1776.

141. The Canadian venture, plus other events around Boston, made it easy to bring about independence, didn't it?

One would think so, but it wasn't so. Many politicians, and others, didn't want to break ties with Great Britain. Pennsylvania, for instance, "strictly enjoined" its delegates to the Continental Congress to reject any proposition "that may cause or lead to a separation from our mother country." Virginia, on the other hand, took an opposite tack. It had Richard Henry Lee (considered a Mason, but without substantiation) submit a resolution calling for independence. This he did on June 7, 1776.

142. Who were the Freemasons who were appointed to the committee to draft a constitution?

Benjamin Franklin of Pennsylvania, a Past Grand Master, and Robert R. Livingston, who would become the first Grand Master of Masons in New York. John Adams and Thomas Jefferson were not Masons. Roger Sherman is claimed by some to have been a Mason, but there is no evidence to substantiate this.

143. After many, many changes the constitutional committee presented its results. What happened?

The oath of secrecy was fully followed. What is known today wasn't revealed for several years. From Jefferson's autobiography we learn the delegates, on July 1, 1776, were almost, but not quite, unanimously in favor of independence. The delegates from Delaware were divided. The discussion, taking place in a committee of the whole, was postponed until the following day. A messenger was sent to Caesar Rodney, the third Delaware delegate. Over horrendous trails, made even more treacherous by torrential rains, Rodney rode the 80 miles through the night. He staggered into Independence Hall in time to turn Delaware's vote in favor of independence. With the change in the vote of South Carolina and Pennsylvania, and the abstinence of New York, the ballot was unanimous! Caesar Rodney died eight years later of cancer. He was not a Mason, but a nephew of the same name was. In 1975 Jenkin Lloyd Jones wrote: "Paul Revere [a Massachusetts Freemason] had a great press agent—Henry Wadsworth Longfellow. Caesar Rodney had no press agent nor was he turned to romantic imagery. But Longworth's line, 'The fate of a nation was riding that night,' could better have been applied to the muddy gentleman from Delaware who dashed to Philadelphia."

144. Is it true that the day for the declaring of independence should be July 2 instead of the 4th?

Perhaps. The 2nd is the day the deed was done, but Jefferson claims the debate continued through July 4th.

145. It is claimed the year 1776 proved disastrous for Washington and his troops. Why?

Among other things, Washington didn't have the forces necessary to make a concerted stand against the British. Toward the end of the year, with morale low, The Commander was forced to retreat into Pennsylvania. In a panic, the Congress fled from Philadelphia.

146. What helped restore some of the morale of the Continental forces?

In the *Pennsylvania Journal* of December 19, 1776, a tract called "The Crisis" by Thomas Paine (not a Mason) appeared. His opening lines have been repeated hundreds of times since, but never did they do as much good as when Washington had the article read to his troops. "These are the times that try men's souls. The summer soldier and the sunshine patriot will, in this crisis, shrink from the service of his country; but he that stands it now deserves the love and thanks of man and woman. Tyranny, like hell, is not easily conquered; yet we have this consolation with us—that the harder the conflict, the more glorious the triumph."

147. Late in December of 1776, Washington planned to score a great coup. What was it?

John Sullivan, who would become the first Grand Master of Masons in New Hampshire, arrived in Washington's camp with 2,000 of the Continental General Charles Lee's men. (Lee had been captured while sleeping in a tavern in Morristown, New Jersey, which some historians consider a blessing!) This reinforced a plan Washington had been considering—to strike the British when and where they believed they were safe—in Trenton!

148. What did Washington do on Christmas night in 1776?

He and his men crossed the Delaware River! What an officer wrote in his diary should be perpetuated: "It will be a terrible night for the soldiers who have no shoes. Some of them have tied old rags around their feet, but I have not heard a man complain." The wind howled, chunks of ice filled the river, conditions were indeed appalling. But Washington relied on the hardy deep-water fishermen from Massachusetts who had on several occasions proved their courage and audacity. They were under the command of Colonel John Glover, a charter member of Philanthropic Lodge in Massachusetts. The horrible weather caused the crossing to take three hours longer than planned, but the Marblehead seamen did the job without losing a man or gun!

149. What happened after the Delaware was crossed?

In a two pronged attack on Trenton, New Jersey, Nathaniel Greene (believed to be a Rhode Island Mason), and Sullivan, the New Hampshire Mason, took the Hessians by surprise. Within a half hour they surrendered. Forty of them were killed, 918 taken prisoner, but 400 of them escaped. Four Americans were killed and four wounded. The guns captured by the Mason, Henry Knox, and the valor of the men under the command of the Virginia Mason, Hugh Mercer, helped bring about the victory with the loss of so few Colonists.

150. Was Washington satisfied after the victory at Trenton?

Not exactly. He offered a bounty of $10 in hard currency (his own money because the Congress wouldn't provide it) for any of his men who would stay beyond the termination of their enlistment. He again crossed the Delaware during the night of December 30-31. Escaping a trap set by Cornwallis, Washington's forces whipped the British at Princeton.

151. While in winter quarters around Morristown, New Jersey, what important event took place?

Foreign officers, many of them Freemasons, joined the Continental forces. Among them was Friedrich Wilhelm von Steuben, who would whip Washington's men into a top-notch fighting force. Thaddeus Kosciuzko came with Benjamin Franklin's recommendation and would become a colonel of engineers. Interestingly, a Lodge in New York City was named for him in 1928; at that time it was the only Polish Lodge in the world. Franklin also sent another Pole, Count Casimir Pulaski, to join the Continentals. Whether or not he was a Mason is debatable, but a Lodge in Chicago was named in his honor, and so is one in Vermont.

152. When did the Marquis de Lafayette join Washington's forces?

In early 1777 at Morristown. Washington and Lafayette would become as father and son during the trying days to follow. Exhaustive research proves Lafayette, in his late teens when he came to America, had already been made a Mason in France. This was proven when he was unanimously elected as an affiliated member of Lodge of *St. Jean d'Ecosse du Contrat Social*, and honor which Lafayette accepted in person on June 24, 1782.

153. Was it true that Washington wouldn't give Lafayette a command until he became a Freemason?

Absolutely false. In 1875 the then Grand Master in Delaware, George Chaytor, claimed Lafayette had said Washington did not have sufficient confidence in him to entrust him with a separate command until he became a Mason. This was an untruth attributed to Lafayette by Chautor, but it was widely circulated (and still is!). Washington, and undoubtedly no one else, knew that Lafayette was a French Mason when the Commander-in-Chief gave him an independent command two weeks before the Continentals went into winter quarters at Valley Forge.

154. Benedict Arnold, the Connecticut Freemason, has been condemned since the traitorous episode at West Point. Did he serve this country well in the earlier days of the War?

There are many unbiased historians (including me—also see the works of Kenneth Roberts and others) who believe he saved the Colonies. He fought a holding action against the British on Lake Champlain. When the British, under the command of John Burgoyne, captured Ticonderoga and continued into the wilds of New York, the American General Schuyler needed help. Washington sent Generals Arnold and Benjamin Lincoln (who would become a member of St. Andrew's Lodge in Boston in 1780) to reinforce the meager American troops. Later, using subterfuge, Arnold caused the Indians working with the British to desert, thereby lifting the siege of Fort Stanwix. Arnold, persuading the indecisive Horatio Gates to let him and his men fight, along with Morgan, whipped the British at Saratoga. This gave Benjamin Franklin the ammunition he needed to convince the French to assist the Americans—an act that would eventually cement the formation of the republic called the United States of America.

Forming A Republic   49

155. Valley Forge in 1778 was a low point in War for American Independence, but were there any redeeming factors?

Some. The Prussian Mason, Baron von Steuben, turned the Continentals into a fighting force. Among other things, he taught them the use of the bayonet. This would help blunt the English advantage in later battles. About the only English language he knew was profanity which he used to good effect. This, along with his good humor, caused his men to drill vigorously. Another advantage was that the Congress finally listened to the advice of Washington. It appointed the Mason, Nathanael Greene as Quartermaster General. Greene wouldn't accept the position until Washington persuaded him take the office so that needed reforms in that department would be carried out.

156. Was all the fighting taking place in the East?

Much of it. But the Virginia Mason, George Rogers Clark, convinced Virginia's Governor Patrick Henry (not a Mason) to take a force westward to blunt the advances of the British. Clark and his 200 "Long Knives" won their first goal, Kaskaskia, on the Mississippi, about 50 miles from St. Louis. British Colonel Henry Hamilton took Vincennes in Indiana. In the dead of winter, with the Wabash River flooded and choked with ice, and only able to travel the last nine miles in a week, Clark and his 127 backwoodsmen, whipped the English on February 25, 1779. Vincennes and the border settlements were finally free.

157. What was happening in Freemasonry during these early years of the War?

Freemasonry remained somewhat active. For instance, in Virginia in 1777 a committee met several times to determine if Virginia should elect its own Grand Master and form a Grand Lodge. This would be accomplished in October 1778. Several Grand Lodges, and Lodges, continued to celebrate the Festivals of the Saints John. American Union Lodge met in various locations whenever possible. Washington moved into Philadelphia on December 22, 1778 and was able to celebrate the Festival of St. John the Evangelist with Pennsylvania and military Masons.

158. Was George Washington elected a General Grand Master?

No. He was seriously proposed for this non-existent position, however. In 1779 the American forces went into winter quarters at Morristown, New Jersey. There American Union Lodge met on December 15. During this meeting the Lodge proposed Washington for General Grand Master. Five days later the Grand Lodge of Pennsylvania did the same! American Union, with Washington present, celebrated the Festival of St. John the Evangelist on the 27th.

159. What is some of the background of American Union Lodge?

Briefly: A group of Masons petitioned John Rowe, the Provincial Grand Master of the Provincial Grand Lodge of Massachusetts for a warrant to form a lodge. Rowe, a Loyalist, had virtually turned control over to his Deputy, Richard Gridley. Gridley readily constituted "American Union Lodge, now erected in Roxbury, or wherever your Body shall remove on the Continent of America, provided it is where no Grand Master is appointed." This wording is important. It permitted the Lodge to meet virtually anywhere. In 1776 it met 31 times, but where isn't always stated. Only one meeting is recorded in 1777 and '78; in three months in 1779 it met 18 times.

160. What happened to American Union Lodge after the end of the War?

Amazingly, it is still in existence! At the urging of several Freemasons at Marietta, Ohio, Jonathan Heart, who had the charter of the Lodge, opened American Union Lodge in that settlement on June 28, 1790. It became No. 1 on the roster of the Grand Lodge of Ohio when that Grand Lodge was organized.

169. It is claimed a Masonic chest was captured by American forces when they stormed Stony Point on July 15, 1779. Is this true, and if so what happened to it?

It's true. It belonged to Lodge Unity No. 18 of the 17th British Regiment. Samuel H. Parsons, the second Master of American Union Lodge, had the chest returned to the regiment. Through a letter to the Grand Lodge of Pennsylvania, Lodge Unity thanked General Parsons.

170. Wasn't the paraphernalia of another British Masonic Lodge returned after its capture?

Forming A Republic   51

There were probably several Masonic items returned of which there are no records. Gould does record one more, however. He said the Masonic chest of the 46th fell into the hands of the Americans. (This was the 46th Foot with warrant No.227, Irish Constitution.) Washington, according to Gould, had "a guard of honor ... take charge of the chest, with other articles of value belonging to the 46th, and return them to the regiment."

171. The forces in the East were stalemated in late 1780 and the early months of 1781; in the South the British were whipping the Continentals. What did General Washington do?

He was finally able to have the Congress listen to and accept his advice, but it wasn't until after General Horatio Gates, appointed by the Congress as Commander of the Southern Army, was soundly defeated (again) on August 16, 1780. At Washington's urging, the Masons, Nathanael Greene and the Baron von Steuben, were selected to salvage the South. They, along with General Daniel Morgan, helped bring about the final major battle of the War at Yorktown, Virginia.

172. How was it learned that the Mason, Benedict Arnold, had become a traitor?

John André, a British spy, was captured near Tarrytown, New York, on September 23, 1780. Papers found on him proved Arnold was selling out his country. Washington is reported to have said when he learned of Arnold's treason: "Whom now can we trust?" André was hanged; Arnold escaped to later play havoc in the South.

173. Did the French help bring about the victory at Yorktown?

Indeed they did! The defeat of the British in the South by Greene, Morgan and von Steuben drove Cornwallis' forces into Virginia in August. Rochambeau and his French troops had joined Washington at White Plains. Shortly thereafter de Grasse "borrowed" 3,000 soldiers from the French commander in Santo Domingo (he had to return them by October 15!). He urged Washington to "employ me promptly and usefully" as he set sail for the Chesapeake, where he arrived on August 28. Lafayette had the British bottled up in Yorktown. He was told by Washington, who was at White Plains, to prevent, at all costs, any escape by the British. Washington, along with the well dressed and armed French soldiers under Rochambeau, out-foxed the English and left for Yorktown. They joined Lafayette on September 11; Admiral Barras with his French fleet had arrived on the 9th.

174. When did Lord Cornwallis surrender?

On October 19, 1781. On the 17th he had asked for a cessation of hostilities.

175. Were there Freemasons involved in the Yorktown episode?

Without question. The British, French and Americans all had some regiments with traveling warrants. But contrary to some reports, there were no known Masonic meetings during this whole period. Among other things, there wasn't time for such gatherings. Yorktown Lodge No. 9 had been revitalized in 1780, but there is absolutely no record of it meeting during this period. Some years later someone, evidently trying to enhance the image of the Craft, claimed a meeting was held, but that was a falsehood. Among the general officers who were Freemasons who were at Yorktown were Henry Knox, Benjamin Lincoln, John P.G. Muhlenberg, Arthur St. Clair and Baron Friedrich W.A. von Steuben. Others included Elias Dayton, Louis le Begue Duportail, Evans, Jonathan Heart, Scammell, John Laurens, George Weeton and William Woodford, and, of course, Marquis de Lafayette and George Washington. In Williamsburg was John Blair, Jr., Grand Master of Masons in Virginia. Rochambeau's army, with at least two traveling Lodges, wintered in Williamsburg.

176. Were all American Freemasons Patriots?

No! Nor were all citizens of the colonies Patriots. More Lodges than we know about were divided down the middle. This appeared to be especially true in New York. Hundreds of Tories (English sympathizers) fled to England, and also Canada. In many instances American Masons established Masonic Lodges in Canada; others affiliated with established Lodges. Truthfully, it was George Washington and a handful of "rabble in arms" who made it possible for what is called a republic and the United States of America.

177. Who were the Freemasons who signed the Declaration of Independence?

The answer to this question is probably the most misunderstood subject in all of Freemasonry. Two men, the late Ronald E. Heaton of Pennsylvania and the late James R. Case of Connecticut (both Fellows of The Philalethes Society) spent a life-time researching and reporting on Freemasonry during the Revolutionary period. Their unbiased results can be found in The Masonic Service Association under the title of *Masonic Membership of the Founding Fathers*. No other purported list should be considered accurate without exhaustive research. NINE OF THE SIGNERS OF THE DECLARATION OF INDEPENDENCE WERE FREEMASONS, OR WOULD BECOME FREEMASONS. They were: William Ellery of Rhode Island (First Lodge of Boston, 1748); Benjamin Franklin of Pennsylvania (St. John's Lodge, Philadelphia, 1731, Grand Master, 1734); John Hancock of Massachusetts (Merchants Lodge No. 277, Quebec, St. Andrew's Lodge, Boston, 1762); Joseph Hewes of North Carolina (Unanimity Lodge No. 7 visited in 1776 [records lost]); William Hooper of North Carolina (Hanover Lodge, NC, 1780 [now extinct]) ; Robert Treat Paine of Massachusetts (attended Grand Lodge, June 26, 1759, Massachusetts [records of membership lost, according to Case]); Richard Stockton of New Jersey (first Master of St. John's Lodge, Princeton, 1765); George Walton of Georgia (Solomon's Lodge No. 1, Savannah, ? [said to have taken degrees a second time in 1785]); William Whipple of New Hampshire (St. John's Lodge, Portsmouth, 1752). It should be noted that by the standards of 1993, the Masonic affiliation of three of these would be considered "suspect."

178. Who were the Freemasons who signed The Articles of Association?

There were ten—and no more. Again according to Heaton and Case they were: Edward Biddle, Richard Caswell, John Dickinson, Joseph Hewes, William Hooper, Charles Humphreys, Robert Treat Paine, Peyton Randolph, John Sullivan and George Washington.

179. The Articles of Confederation were approved by the Congress on July 9, 1778. Who were the Freemasons who signed these Articles?

There were nine. Thomas Adams, Daniel Carroll, John Dickinson, William Ellery, John Hancock, Cornelius Harnett, Henry Laurens, Daniel Roberdeau, Jonathan Bayard Smith. It should be noted that signatures were added until May 9, 1779. But it wasn't until February 7, 1781 that the last of the states (Maryland) agreed to the Articles.

It should also be noted, these Articles gave the Congress little, if any, power. One of the problems George Washington had to contend with was the lack of unity among the colonies. Another was the lack of meaningful decisions by members of the Congresses.

180. Who were the Presidents of the Continental Congresses who were Freemasons?

   Peyton Randolph of Virginia, 1774 and again in 1775 (he died October 22, 1775); John Hancock of Massachusetts, 1775 and again in 1785 (but couldn't serve in '85 because of ill health); Henry Laurens of South Carolina, 1777; Arthur St. Clair of Pennsylvania, 1787.

181. How many Freemasons signed the Constitution of the United States, and who were they?

   There were 13, namely: Gunning Bedford, Jr. of Delaware; John Blair, Jr. of Virginia; David Brearly of New Jersey; Jacob Broom of Delaware; Daniel Carroll of Maryland; Jonathan Dayton of New Jersey; John Dickinson of Pennsylvania and Delaware; Benjamin Franklin of Pennsylvania; Nicholas Gilman of New Hampshire; Rufus King of Massachusetts; James McHenry of Maryland; William Paterson of New Jersey; George Washington of Virginia.

5. The Influence of George Washington

In all our deliberations on this subject [the Constitution] we kept steadily in our view, that which appears to us the greatest interest of every true American, the consolidation of our Union, in which is involved our prosperity, felicity, safety, perhaps our national existence. This important consideration, seriously and deeply impressed on our minds, led each state in the Convention to be less rigid on points of inferior magnitude, than might have been otherwise expected, and thus the Constitution, which we now present, is the result of a spirit of amity, and of that mutual deference and concession which the peculiarity of our political situation rendered indispensable.

GEORGE WASHINGTON, *President*
Constitutional Convention
September 17, 1787

182. What brought about a Constitutional Convention?

The Articles of Confederation had caused chaos in the United States. Under these articles the Congress had virtually no power. It couldn't levy any taxes. "Taxation without representation" had helped bring about the Revolution, consequently taxation was a no-no. Because a strong central government in Great Britain had caused the people in the colonies to suffer, power was reserved for the states. Each adopted its own constitution, leaving the Congress powerless. The Congress could count only on the good faith of the States. This good faith was practically non-existent.

183. Did this initial action by the States have an effect on Freemasonry in the United States?

Evidently. From the beginning of the Grand Lodge system in the United States to the present day (1994) each Grand Lodge has reserved unto itself exclusive jurisdiction. Each controls its own members, administers its own laws, and collects its own taxes. Each determines which Masonically related bodies it will recognize, and none can function within its jurisdiction without its consent.

183. What helped Freemasonry move westward?

The passing by the Congress of a "Land Ordinance" on May 20, 1785 played an important role in the westward movement. It appeared to have two purposes: to raise money (each building site would cost $640 cash), and to encourage settlement between the Appalachians, the Mississippi and the Ohio. An example of the Masonic movement westward: General Rufus Putnam of American Union Lodge fame (and who would become the first Grand Master of Masons in Ohio) persuaded several veterans to travel from Boston to the Ohio Territory with him. On April 7, 1786 they landed near Fort Harmar. Later they founded Marietta. On June 28, 1790, Jonathan Heart who held the charter of American Union Lodge, called the Lodge to resume its labor. It was the first Masonic Lodge communication held in the Ohio Territory.

184. What were the early Lodges doing in the meantime?

Here it is confirmed that Grand Lodges are the creatures of Craft Lodges. From the first Grand Lodge in 1717 to the more recent formation of Grand Lodges, it took Symbolic Lodges to form them. So it was during the early days in the United States, the established Lodges formed independent Grand Lodges, many of them warranted (or chartered) by Provincial Grand Lodges owing their allegiance to one of the two Grand Lodges in England, or to the Grand Lodge of Scotland. Virginia, whose Lodges owed their allegiance to no one overseas Grand Lodge, became the first to form an independent Grand Lodge. This was consummated on October 13, 1778. In South Carolina the schisms ended and a Grand Lodge was formed on December 27, 1783. Differences were reconciled in Pennsylvania and its Grand Lodge was formed on September 25, 1786. The Grand Lodge of Georgia was formed on December 16, 1786; New Jersey on December 18, 1786; Maryland, April 19, 1787 (this completed work started in 1783); New York, June 6, 1787 (but it would be troubled with schisms in later years).

185. When and where did the Constitutional Convention begin?

The Convention was scheduled to start on May 14, 1787, but bad weather and horrible roads kept many of the delegates from arriving on time. It was May 25 before a quorum of seven states arrived to permit the Convention to begin.

186. What part did Freemasonry play in the Convention?

None—contrary to what some have claimed. It's true that individual Freemasons were influential, but as a body Freemasonry didn't control the actions of the delegates. It's true that Edmund Randolph, Governor of Virginia and Grand Master of Masons there, along with Virginia's delegation, drew up a plan of action during the wait for a quorum. It's true that this plan was presented at the opening of the Convention, but it was the work of individuals, not Freemasonry as such.

187. Wasn't a Freemason elected to preside over the Convention?

Yes. George Washington, perhaps the best known and most respected man in the Colonies, was chosen as President of the Convention. His Brother Mason, Benjamin Franklin, planned on placing Washington's name in nomination, but he was ill. It was Robert Morris (not known to be a Mason) who nominated the former Commander-in-Chief, who was unanimously elected.

188. Didn't the delegates adopt an oath of secrecy? If so, how do we know what occurred during the Convention?

Yes, an oath of secrecy was adopted—and kept. Years later, notes recorded by several of the delegates were released. These were compiled in 1927 in *Documents Illustrative of the Formation of the Union of the American States*. Other journals and books published their versions of the events that took place in 1787.

189. What did the delegates agree to do that was Masonic in character?

They didn't form committees but agreed to meet as a Committee of the Whole. This was almost universally done in the early days of the Craft. Today there are but few Masonic bodies acting this wisely.

190. How did one of the delegates (William Pierce of Georgia) who made notes of individuals record his opinion of a few of the Freemasons among the participants?

About **Rufus King**, a member of St. John's Lodge, Massachusetts: "Much distinguished for his eloquence and great parliamentary talents"; **William Patterson**, who would become a Freemason in 1791 in Trenton Lodge No. 9, New Jersey: "A man of great modesty, a classic, a lawyer, and an orator"; **Benjamin Franklin**, a Past Grand Master in Pennsylvania: "The greatest philosopher of the present age, the very heavens obey him, he is no speaker, however, he tells a story in a style most engaging"; **John Dickinson**, member of Lodge No. 18, Delaware: "A scholar, an indifferent speaker, however, a good writer"; **Jacob Broom** of Lodge No. 14, Delaware: "A plain good man, nothing to render him conspicuous, silent in public, but cheerful and conversational in private"; **James McHenry**, would become a member of Spiritual Lodge No. 16, Maryland, in 1806: "Nothing of genius to improve him, no graces of the orator, however, a very remarkable young gentleman"; **Daniel Carroll**, member of Lodge No. 16, Maryland: "A man of large fortune, and influence in his state, possesses plain good sense"; **George Washington,** a member of Fredericksburg Lodge No. 4, and Alexandria No. 22, Virginia: "He may be said to be the deliverer of his country, he appears as the politician and the statesman, and like Cincinnnatus he returned to his farm perfectly content with being only a plain citizen, now only seeks the approbation of his countrymen"; **John Blair, Jr.**, first Grand Master in Virginia: "One of the most respectable men in Virginia, one of the judges of the Supreme Court in Virginia, has a very extensive knowledge of the law, he is no orator, but his good sense and principles compensate for other deficiencies"; **Edmund Randolph**, then Grand Master in Virginia: "A young gentleman in whom unite all the accomplishments of the scholar and statesman, has a most harmonious voice and striking manner."

191. What is the Society of The Cincinnati?

The Society was formed in 1783 with George Washington as its first president. General, and Brother, Henry Knox was its secretary. Many of its members were Freemasons. Its purpose was to provide aid for widows and orphans of those officers who had died during the war. Its membership was restricted to the officers of the Continental Forces and their dependents. It is still in existence.

192. What was the greatest stumbling block the delegates to the Constitutional Convention encountered to developing a Constitution to present to the Congress?

It was the battle between the "small" and "large" states. The impasse was broken when the delegates agreed the government would consist of a Senate that would have two members from each state, regardless of its size, and a House of Representatives that would have delegates according to the population of the state. This would become the legislative branch; the executive branch would be the President.

193. When was the Constitution of the United States finally approved by the Convention and ordered to be engrossed on parchment?

On September 17, 1787. Of the 42 delegates present at the conclusion, 39 signed, three refused, and among the latter was Edmund Randolph of Virginia. But this document would mean nothing unless it was ratified by at least nine states.

194. Edmund Randolph, Virginia's Grand Master, didn't sign the Constitution as presented to the Congress, but what did he do during the ratification process?

He fought for the ratification of the Constitution (see the report under Virginia). It was submitted to the States on September 28, 1787, and the fight for its ratification began.

195. Which were the first States to ratify the Constitution?

Delaware was the first, and would let the world know about this to the present day. It did it on December 7, 1787. Pennsylvania, under the leadership of the Mason Benjamin Franklin, followed five days later. Georgia was next on January 2, 1788; Connecticut on January 9th.

196. With the Freemason John Hancock as President of the Massachusetts Convention, what did it do insofar as ratification was concerned?

It ratified it on February 6, but it added several suggestions for improvement. These would become the basis for the "Bill of Rights" which other States also supported in later months. Hancock was supported by William Cushing, a member of St. Andrew's Lodge, and who would later move to Ohio and become the first Master of Farmer's Lodge No. 20 in Belpre.

197. Did other Freemasons support ratification of the Constitution?

Yes. Among them was George Plater who had served several years as Master of the Lodge at Leonardtown, Maryland. On April 28, 1788 Maryland ratified the Constitution. Oliver Ellsworth who had been the charter Master of St. John's Lodge in Princeton, New Jersey, and a highly respected lawyer in Connecticut, wrote an open letter to the citizens of New Hampshire on March 10, 1788. In this letter he urged them, for their own benefit, to support ratification. On June 21 New Hampshire became the ninth State to support the Constitution. This resulted in making the Constitution a legal and binding document.

198. What happened during the fight for ratification in Virginia?

It was stormy, indeed. The governor, Patrick Henry (NOT a Mason) bitterly opposed ratification. Among those fighting for its adoption were Edmund Randolph, John Marshall, who would later become Grand Master, and Edmund Pendleton, a member of Fairfax Lodge No. 43. The latter came out of retirement to accept the Presidency of the Convention. After a heated denunciation by Henry, Pendleton turned the chair over to someone else, then point by point slashed away at Henry's arguments. The proponents won. On June 26, 1788 Virginia became the tenth State to ratify the Constitution.

199. Who presided over the New York Convention?

Governor George Clinton who would be Master of Warren Lodge No. 17, New York City. His uncle was DeWitt Clinton who would become Grand Master of Masons in New York from 1806 to 1819. New York approved the Constitution on July 28, 1788, but, as other States had, requested several additions be made to it.

200. Didn't a Freemason preside over the North Carolina Convention?

Yes, it was Samuel "Sam" Johnston, the first Grand Master of Masons in North Carolina, serving from 1787 to 1792. The earlier

Convention had postponed ratification hoping several amendments would be made. They weren't, but the Convention approved the Constitution on November 21, 1789. However, it suggested 21 changes be adopted.

201. What happened to Rhode Island in the ratification process?

It had opposed the Constitutional Convention, and it refused to have anything to do with ratification. The federal government, under President Washington, treated Rhode Island as a foreign country and stopped all commerce between it and the United States. The State capitulated, somewhat. On May 9, 1790 it ratified the Constitution, but demanded 21 changes be made immediately! It said it would obey only those provisions the politicians in power in the state believed consistent with the laws of Rhode Island!

202. Did George Washington seek the Presidency of the United States?

On the contrary, Washington wanted to remain at Mount Vernon. Alexander Hamilton (not a Mason), and hundreds of others, urged him to accept the nomination if the electors selected on the first Wednesday of January 1789 chose him for the job. He was the unanimous choice.

203. To accept the Presidency by traveling to New York, what did Washington have to do?

He said he had to do something he "never expected to be driven to, that is, borrow money on Interest." The amount was 500 pounds and was used to clear his accounts at home.

204. There were Masonic episodes during the inauguration on April 30, 1789 in New York City. What were some of them?

The committee had forgotten to provide a Holy Bible. General Jacob Morton, Master of St. John's Lodge No. 1 rushed to his Lodge to get and return with the altar Bible. The Grand Master of Masons in New York, Robert R. Livingston, Chancellor, administered the oath. After the oath, Washington, as he had done when he received the degrees in Fredericksburg Lodge, bowed and kissed the Bible.

205. Was George Washington Master of his Lodge when he assumed the office of President of the United States?

He was. On April 28, 1788 a charter was issued by the Grand Lodge of Virginia for Alexandria Lodge No. 22. It was signed by Grand Master Edmund Randolph. Washington was named first thereby making him the Charter Master. The Lodge elected him Master on December 20, so he was Master when he was installed as President of the United States.

206. When were the ten amendments, to be called "The Bill of Rights," officially added to the Constitution?

Of the 12 amendments submitted, ten were adopted on December 15, 1791. Two of the four signers that placed the resolution of the amendment before the Congress were Freemasons: John Beckley, Clerk of the House of Representatives, was a member of Williamsburg Lodge No. 6, Virginia; Frederick Augustus Muhlenberg, Speaker of the House of Representatives, was a member of Lodge No. 3, Pennsylvania.

207. Who presided at the laying of the boundary-stone of the newly created Federal District?

Dr. Elisha Cullen Dick, Master of Alexandria Lodge No. 22, Virginia, officiated on April 15, 1791. The district was comprised of portions of Alexandria, Virginia, and Georgetown, Maryland. Hundreds of Freemasons joined in the festivities. It was Dr. Dick who stepped aside so that Washington could become Master of Alexandria Lodge.

208. Was the cornerstone of "The President's House," later to be called "The White House," laid with Masonic rites?

It was. The date was November 13, 1792. The only account of this little known event appeared in the *City Gazette* of Charlotte, South Carolina, for the 15th.

209. Who were some of the Freemasons appointed to important governmental posts early in Washington's administration?

Edmund Randolph became Attorney General (later he would

become the Secretary of State); (John Jay, the first Chief Justice of the Supreme Court wrote a graphic letter to Washington using striking Masonic language, but as far as is known, he wasn't a Mason); Henry Knox was appointed as Secretary of War.

210. What were the Masonic connections involved in the laying of the cornerstone of the United States Capitol on September 18, 1793?

The architect for the Capitol was James Hoban, a Roman Catholic and Freemason who, along with others, received a charter for Federal Lodge from the Grand Lodge of Maryland. The procession was led by George Washington's Lodge, Alexandria No.22, along with Lodge No. 9 of Maryland. The President played an important role during the Masonic rites in the laying of the cornerstone. Newspaper reports of the event were glowing. Artists over the years would illustrate their versions of this important event, each of them featuring the President, George Washington, in Masonic regalia.

211. Where in the Capitol is the cornerstone located?

No one knows! Voluntary monetary contributions poured in before the 200th anniversary of this event to aid in a continuing search for the cornerstone laid in 1793. It wasn't found. During the two centuries the Capitol has been expanded, burned, expanded again and again. If the cornerstone had been placed in the northeast corner, it is embedded somewhere in the expanded building. Charles Scala spearheaded an unsuccessful search for the stone in 1992-93. He wanted to continue the search claiming: "It's the closest thing we have to the Holy Grail. In laying that stone, it was the beginning of the process that would ensure the rights of [the] liberty we enjoy." On September 18, 1993 a full scale Masonic reenactment of the cornerstone laying of 200 years earlier took place. Dignitaries, Masonic and political, from all over the country were present.

212. What are some of the important points George Washington stressed in his "Farewell Address" as President of the United States?

This masterful speech should be read in its entirety. Much of it has proven prophetic. Briefly: He stressed the importance of the Constitution and urged all Americans to support it. He warned against political parties, including employing many adjectives to enhance his warning, including "designing men" who would spread "jealousies" and "misrepresentations." He asked the people to support institutions of learning, religion and morality. He warned against "the insidious wiles of foreign influence" and foreign political connections kept at a minimum. Later he urged the Congress to establish a military academy.

213. When John Adams (not a Mason) took office as President, did Washington's service to the country end?

No. An undeclared naval war with France in 1798 appeared to be a reality. Washington was asked to take charge of the army, and a navy department was established. The increase in the number of frigates authorized by the Congress of the United States in 1797 by six, which included the *United States* (launched May 10, 1797) and the still famous *Constellation* (also launched in 1797) brought an end to this threat, and Washington was able to return to his home. Incidentally, the *Constellation* was a flagship of the Atlantic fleet during World War II! It served longer than any other ship, and is now preserved in Baltimore.

214. What caused the death of George Washington?

Washington developed a severe sore throat on December 12, 1799. Dr. James Craik, a member of Washington's Lodge, was called, but was unable to save the former President. He died close to eleven o'clock on the evening of December 14.

215. Was Washington buried with Masonic rites?

He was. On the afternoon of December 18, 1799 pall bearers, all colonels, and all Freemasons except one, carried Washington's body to the vault at Mount Vernon. There Dr. Elisha Cullen Dick, Master of Alexandria Lodge No. 22, conducted the Masonic ceremonies.

216. What did John Marshall, the Virginia Mason, tell the House of Representatives on the day of Washington's funeral?

"Our Washington is no more! the hero, the patriot, and the sage of America;... the man on whom in times of danger, every eye turned and all hopes were placed ... lives now only in his own great actions, and in the hearts of an affectionate and afflicted people."

6. Growth of American Freemasonry

Under the Constitution and with the guidance of such great men and Freemasons as Washington ... and Marshall, the States ... unified and prospered. Clearly, here was a new nation based on high principles and eager to make its way in the world.... It soon became evident to men of foresight that America's manifest destiny was to reach from sea to sea.
Henry C. Clausen
Masons Who Helped Shape Our Nation

217. When did Freemasonry enter Vermont?

On September 18, 1758, after the surrender of Quebec, a Military Lodge held a meeting in Vermont. Five Military Lodges, four of them under Irish registry, held a joint meeting on November 18, 1758. But it would be three years before a settlement, Bennington, was established in what would become Vermont on March 4, 1791. Because it was "open territory," Lodges formed there received charters from Massachusetts, Connecticut and the Provincial Grand Lodge of Quebec. The latter chartered Dorchester Lodge in Vergennes, Vermont in 1791. On October 14, 1794 a constitution was adopted and Grand Lodge officers elected.

218. Where did the Lodges in what would become Kentucky receive their charters?

From the Grand Lodge of Virginia, inasmuch as the territory was a part of the Old Dominion. On November 17, 1788 Lexington Lodge became No. 25 on the roster of the Grand Lodge of Virginia. Four other Lodges would be warranted by Virginia, including Abraham, the Lodge that buried George Rogers Clark with Masonic rites. Kentucky was admitted to the union on June 1, 1792. Grand Lodge officers were elected on October 1, 1800 bringing into being the Grand Lodge of Kentucky.

219. Why did Tripoli declare war on the United States?

Bribes had been paid to the Barbary States for years to keep American shipping from being raided along the coast of North Africa. In 1801 the Pasha of Tripoli demanded larger sums. He received no immediate answer, so he declared war. Commodore Edward Preble, made a Mason in St. Andrew's Lodge of Boston and who became a member of Portland Lodge No. 17, with little help from the Congress, led the naval forces to a quick victory.

220. Who negotiated the purchase of the Louisiana Territory?

Robert Livingston, a New York Mason, and James Monroe, a Virginia Mason, on orders from President Jefferson made the French an offer for the purchase of New Orleans. All were shocked when they were offered the whole of the Louisiana Territory. For fifteen million dollars the size of the United States was doubled! The American flag was raised over the Territory on December 20, 1803.

221. Who were commissioned to explore the wilderness from Missouri to the Pacific Ocean?

Captain Meriwether Lewis, who received his Masonic degrees in Door of Virtue Lodge in Virginia, and later became a charter member of St. Louis Lodge No. 111, Missouri, as did his partner, Captain William Clark (brother of George Rogers Clark). They started up the Missouri River on May 14, 1803, reached the Pacific Ocean, and the expedition returned to Missouri on September 23, 1806.

222. When was the Grand Lodge of Delaware established?

In 1806, by Lodges holding charters from the Provincial Grand Lodge of Pennsylvania.

223. Who was the first Grand Master of Masons in Ohio, and when was he elected?

Rufus Putnam of American Union Lodge was elected Grand Master on January 9, 1808.

224. What Ohio Mason became the first Grand Master in Michigan?

Lewis Cass was elected the third Grand Master in Ohio and became the first Grand Master in Michigan in 1829. However, this Grand Lodge bowed to the anti-Masonic fiasco then running rampant, and didn't function. It was 1841 before it resumed labor and Levi Cook, who refused to serve, was elected Grand Master.

225. Who were among the Freemasons who demanded war against the British after the Battle of Tippecanoe in November 1811?

Henry Clay, Speaker of the House, and who would become Grand Master of Masons in Kentucky in 1820, along with General Andrew Jackson, who would become Grand Master of Masons in Tennessee from 1822-24. (Tennessee had been admitted to the union on June 1, 1796.) They believed there was proof that the British were arming Indians to fight against Americans. Tecumseh (Shooting Star), a great Shawnee chief, was defeated in this battle by the anti-Mason, General William Henry Harrison.

226. When was a Grand Lodge formed in the District of Columbia?

On January 11, 1811 Grand Lodge officers were elected. This was the culmination of discussions that had gone on for several years. The Grand Lodge was composed mainly of Maryland Lodges. Alexandria Lodge refused to break away from Virginia.

227. When was war declared against Great Britain?

On June 18, 1812, but the vote was close: 79 to 49 in the House; 19 to 13 in the Senate. The slight majority caused as many problems then as would be experienced 150 years later during the war (or police action) in Vietnam.

228. What did General Stephen Van Rensselaer do in October, 1812?

He resigned in disgust! With 200 men he had ferried the Niagara River and attacked Queenston Heights, paving the way for the New York militia to follow. The militia refused to cross from the American side. Van Rensselaer, who would become Grand Master of Masons in New York from 1825 to 1829, quit in disgust because of the cowardice of his countrymen.

229. What wretched act took place in the District of Columbia in 1814?

The President's House was torched on August 24th by British troops as American militia broke and ran; so did the politicians! Dolly Madison, the President's wife, grabbed a full-length painting of George Washington and ran to join those who had ran across the Potomac. After the House was repaired, it was whitewashed to cover the smoke damage. Ever after it became known as "the White House."

230. Who won the "War of 1812"?

No one! Toward the end of 1814 the "Treaty of Ghent" was signed. It specified that neither side had won or lost!

231. Did the acceptance of the treaty end the war?

Not exactly. General Andrew Jackson, the Freemason, two weeks after the treaty was signed, defeated the British in a major battle in New Orleans.

232. Who helped finance much of the cost of the War of 1812?

There are those who believe Stephen Girard, a member of Royal Arch Lodge No. 4, Pennsylvania, spearheaded the financing of the war. Politicians in 1811 refused to recharter the Bank of the United States, thereby creating the strong possibility of financial ruin. Girard founded another bank for the country, and made five million dollars available to the government. He willed most of his fortune to found Girard College in Philadelphia, specifying the students be taught no sect.

233. What two Grand Lodges were formed during the War of 1812?

Louisiana's five French-speaking Lodges elected Grand Lodge officers on June 20, 1812. (The two English-speaking Lodges refused to participate.) The Grand Lodge of Tennessee came into being on December 27, 1813.

234. What did the Freemason, Stephen Decatur, Jr., say after his squadron had defeated Algeria in 1815?

"Our country! In her intercourse with foreign countries may she always be in the right; but our country, right or wrong!"

235. When was the Grand Lodge of Indiana formed?

Grand Lodge officers were elected on January 13, 1816. One of the most famous, and knowledgeable Freemasons to come out of this Grand Lodge was Dwight L. Smith. Smith was born in 1909, died in 1993. He was made a Freemason in 1934. In 1945 he served Indiana as its Grand Master, and was its Grand Secretary from 1947 to 1979. In the meantime he was the editor of its Masonic magazine, President and Fellow of The Philalethes Society, and was an original member of The Masonic Brotherhood of the Blue Forget-Me-Not. He wrote several books, and received many Masonic honors.

236. Who was Thomas Smith Webb? What was his connection with the General Grand Chapter of Royal Arch Masons?

Briefly, Webb has been called the "Father of the American Rite of Freemasonry." Among other things, he took the work of Preston (see earlier report) and "Americanized" it. In 1816 Webb became the Deputy of the newly elected General Grand High Priest, DeWitt Clinton.

237. What is some of the early history of the General Grand Chapter, Royal Arch Masons?

It was formed by the chapters from New England and New York in 1798. That same year Grand Chapters were formed in New England and New York. In 1806 it was named the "General Grand Chapter of Royal Arch Masons of the United States of America." The "United States" was dropped in 1954, and "International" was added.

238. When was a Grand Lodge formed in Mississippi?

Mississippi became the 20th state on December 10, 1817. On July 27, 1818 it elected Grand Lodge officers.

239. Who was Joel R. Poinsett?

His name is memorialized around Christmas every year, although most don't realize this. He was sent to Mexico in 1822, and in 1825 he returned to that country as a United States Minister. While there he established five Masonic Lodges whose charters were granted by the Grand Lodge of New York. These Lodges later formed the Grand Lodge of Mexico. For 20 years he served as Grand High Priest in South Carolina. He served as Secretary of War from 1837 to 1841, which prevented him from serving as Grand Master of that jurisdiction. But why is he memorialized every Christmas? Because he brought to South Carolina a plant which he developed into the *Poinsettia pulcherrima*—commonly called the "poinsettia."

240. When was the Grand Lodge of Maine formed?

Organized Freemasonry entered Maine in 1762 when it was a part of Massachusetts. Maine became the 23rd state to be admitted to the Union on March 15, 1820. Months earlier representatives met to discuss the formation of a Grand Lodge. On June 1, 1820 Grand Lodge officers were elected. One of the most prominent Past Grand Masters to serve this jurisdiction was Josiah Hayden Drummond.

241. Which Grand Lodge chartered the Lodges that formed the Grand Lodge of Missouri?

Tennessee chartered the three Lodges that met to form the Grand Lodge of Missouri. This was done on May 4, 1821. As with most Grand Lodges, many prominent men served as Grand Masters. Among them were two excellent authors, a father and son, Ray V. and William R. Denslow. Then there was President Harry S. Truman who served his Grand Lodge as Grand Master while he was a Senator. (For his unusual Masonic record see *Brother Truman*.)

242. When was the Grand Lodge of Alabama formed?

On June 16, 1821. Its early Lodges had received charters from five different Grand Lodges.

243. What important doctrine did the Freemason who was President of the United States establish in 1823?

James Monroe, in an address to the Congress, warned all nations to observe the independence of all nations in the hemisphere. This became known as the "Monroe Doctrine."

244. The 1824 election found a non-Mason opposing two Freemasons. Who were they?

Henry Clay and Andrew Jackson were the Freemasons; John Quincy Adams was the other. No candidate received a majority. Clay threw his support to Adams in the House, so Adams became the President.

245. When was John Marshall appointed to the United States Supreme Court?

John Marshall served as Chief Justice of the nation's Supreme Court from 1801 until his death in 1835, a total of 34 years. He had served as Grand Master of Masons in Virginia in 1793, although he had never served as the Master of a Lodge. In spite of his busy schedule he remained an active Freemason throughout his adult life. In the oldest Masonic Hall in the United States he received the Marquis de Lafayette on October 30, 1824, during the latter's triumphal tour of the country. John Dove, another Virginia Masonic stalwart, officiated at the Masonic rites for the burial of Marshall on July 9, 1835.

246. Is there a list of Supreme Court Justices who were Freemasons?

Ronald E. Heaton, a Fellow of The Philalethes Society, compiled a list of Supreme Court Justices who were Freemasons. Of the original six Justices, two were Freemasons: William Cushing of Massachusetts and John Blair, Jr., of Virginia. In 1869 the number of Justices was set at nine (eight plus a Chief Justice). Through 1968 there were 96 who served on the Court. Of these, 39 were known to be Freemasons: Henry Baldwin, Hugo L. Black, John Blair, Jr., Samuel Blatchford, Harold H. Burton, James F. Byrnes, John Catton, Thomas C. Clark, John H. Clarke, William Cushing, William O. Douglas, Oliver Ellsworth, Stephen J. Field, John M. Harlan, Robert H. Jackson, Joseph R. Lamar, John Marshall, Stanley Mathews, Sherman

Minton, William H. Moody, Samuel Nelson, William Paterson, Mahlon Pitney, Stanley F. Reed, Wiley B. Rutledge, Potter Stewart, Noah H. Swayne, William H. Taft, Thomas Todd, Robert Trimble, Willis Van Devanter, Frederick M. Vinson, Earl Warren, Levi Woodbury, and William B. Woods. In 1967 Thurgood Marshal, a Prince Hall Mason, was appointed to the Court. Since then no Freemason has been considered for membership on this court.

7. Bigots Ferociously Malign the Craft

...let me state that I am not and never have been a Roman Catholic .... I just could not believe that this was a book that had shaken up a government. It had shaken me up, but for a totally different reason, I was awestruck that Mr. [Stephen] Knight could summon up from some great reservoir of chutzpah the testicular diameter required to identify himself in The Brotherhood as a "neutral observer." After all, if a "neutral observer" asserts accusations of unfair advancement in business and government, corruption of the police and the judicial system, a connection with the KGB, an infiltration of the Vatican in a conspiracy to commit the biggest financial fraud of our time, responsibility for the Jack the Ripper murders, and the undoubted worship of the Devil, what is left for an enemy to assert?

John J. Robinson
in *Born in Blood: The Lost Secrets of Freemasonry*

247. For what is Batavia, New York, famous (or infamous)?

It's where what was to become known as the "Morgan Affair" began in 1826.

248. What was the "Morgan Affair"?

It was an additional excuse for those who hated Freemasonry to continue their attempts to destroy the Fraternity. Briefly: The story began when a fellow named William Morgan moved to Batavia in 1824. He claimed he was a Freemason, and had been a captain in the War of 1812. Both were outright lies. But somehow he had learned enough about the ritual of the Craft to be accepted as a visitor. He was even Exalted a Royal Arch Mason in Western Star Chapter No. 35 at LeRoy, New York, although no one has ever learned where he received the degrees making him eligible to receive the Royal Arch Degree. He was among the signers of a petition to form a chapter in Batavia, but for some reason his name was deleted. This made him furious. He entered into a partnership with the publisher of a newspaper to release "an exposition of Ancient Craft Masonry, by one who has been a member of the institution for years." A few Freemasons, for some reason, didn't want this published. Eventually Morgan was arrested for unpaid debts. On September 12, 1826 the jailer's wife accepted the payment of the debts and released him to his unknown benefactor. Morgan was seen to enter a closed carriage. It was said he was conveyed to Fort Niagara from which he disappeared.

249. What happened to William Morgan?

No one knows, or at least, no one can honestly say they know. Many wild, but unfounded and unproven, claims were made. In fact, they continue to be made. Unscrupulous politicians, religious bigots, and others who hated Freemasonry have claimed Morgan was murdered by Freemasons, but no evidence of this has ever been discovered.

250. Didn't William Morgan become a martyr to the cause of anti-Masonry?

He did. At the Old Elmwood Cemetery in Batavia, New York, a monument was dedicated in the name of Morgan on September 13, 1882. (an indication that anti-Masonry was continuing.) It is said money was collected to build and place it from Canada and 26 of the States. An anti-Masonic convention was held for three days at the time of the dedication, and about 1,000 attended. (The small number would indicate the bigots were not overly strong.)

251. What was written on the Morgan monument?

On the south side: "Sacred to the memory of William Morgan, a respectable citizen of Batavia and a martyr to the freedom of writing and printing the truth. He was abducted from near this spot in the year 1826 by The Free Masons [sic] and murdered [sic] for revealing the secrets of their order." Strange. He was considered a derelict (among other things) during his stay in the area. The inscription of the east side reads: "Erected by volunteer contributions from over 2000 persons residing in Canada, Ontario, and twenty-six of the United

States and Territories." The north side: "The Court records of Genesee County and the Files of The Batavia Advocate kept in the recorder's office contain the history of the events that caused the erection of this monument." The west side: "The ban of our civil institutions is to be found in Masonry, already powerful and daily becoming more so ** I owe to my Country an exposure of its dangers. Capt. [sic] Wm. Morgan." (There is no record of Morgan ever earning the designation of "captain" or any other legitimate title.)

252. What helped agitate the anti-Masonic agitation?

A non-Mason's account is written in *Freemasonry in American History*: "Charles McCarthy's 'The Antimasonic Party' is perhaps the best treatise on the subject even though it was written in 1902. He concluded the opposition to Freemasonry evolved from several factors. Many of the opponents were envious of the 'wealthy, influential' and 'aristocratic men' who were Freemasons. There were religious 'leaders' who desired much more influence in some political party. Some politicians were seeking a cause, no matter what or who was harmed, to get themselves elected. Religion, bias, and politics gave the anti-Masons their strength. But this strength was confined, mainly, to the rural areas."

253. How badly was Freemasonry harmed by the anti-Masonic furor that began in 1826?

Thousands of pages have been written to cover the horrors suffered for more than a decade of persecution of Freemasonry and Freemasons. Briefly: In New York the 480 Lodges in 1827 dwindled to 82 in 1830; the membership decreased from 20,000 to 3,000. In Vermont the Grand Lodge went out of existence for several years (but three Grand Lodge officers supposedly met biennially). Michigan formed a Grand Lodge but it was abandoned quickly. In Maine, Lodges meeting at Grand Lodge decreased year by year until in 1842 none were represented.

254. Why were a few anti-Masons able to almost abolish as large an organization as Freemasonry?

(An opinion question, but the answer is based on years of searching for an explanation.) From the beginning of the Grand Lodge system in 1717 (at least) the Masonic leadership has turned its back on its critics. It has taken the position of refusing to answer criticism of any kind. This went on in England until the publication of an obviously fabricated anti-Masonic book in 1984. From that point on the Grand Lodge changed its earlier attitude. In the United States the Masonic leadership didn't react to the anti-Masonic tirades until bigots within the Southern Baptist Convention in 1992 attacked Freemasonry. This caused the leadership to take a different tack. In the 1830s it wasn't until a few leaders in Rhode Island and Pennsylvania fought the critics that their anti-Masonic "crusade" was broken.

255. Would Morgan's contemplated exposure of Freemasonry be the first ever published?

Absolutely not. Exposés of Freemasonry, in some form, have been around since before the beginning of the Grand Lodge system in 1717. In 1730 Samuel Prichard's *Masonry Dissected*, the best known of all of them, was circulated in both the New and Old Worlds. *Three Distinct Knocks* appeared in England in 1760. Two years later *Jachin and Boaz* appeared. Legitimate Masonic scholars can be thankful for these publications; they provide the only information available about the rituals, and customs, of those periods. (See the Bibliography for books with information about "The Morgan Affair".)

256. Were there any "legitimate" Masonic publications prior to 1826?

William Preston, an Englishman, became a Freemason in 1762, and immediately began a search for Masonic information. In 1775 he published his *Illustrations of Masonry*. It contained an authentic account of the lectures and ceremonies of the Fraternity. It was widely circulated. Other legitimate Masonic books were those containing Grand Lodge constitutions published by them.

257. Did Preston's book find its way to the United States?

It did. And it was "Americanized" by Thomas Smith Webb in 1797 as *Illustrations of Masonry* or *Freemasons' Monitor*.

258. Who was Thomas Smith Webb?

Webb has been termed the "Father of American, or York Rite Freemasonry." He was born October 13, 1771 in Boston, Massachusetts; died July 6, 1819 during a visit to Cleveland, Ohio. He was

Grand Master of Masons in Rhode Island in 1813. In 1799, when the General Grand Chapter of Royal Arch Masons assumed this name, Webb became its General Grand Scribe. He became General Grand High Priest in 1816. He established the Grand Chapters of Ohio and Kentucky. It's his *Monitor* for which he is remembered.

259. Did Freemasonry come to a complete impasse during the anti-Masonic period?

The greatest damage occurred in the East and in those states where New Englanders, in particular, had migrated, such as Ohio and Michigan. The South, for the most part, ignored (or didn't know about) the enemies of Freemasonry in the North and East. The Grand Lodge of Florida was formed on July 9, 1830. Texas won its independence from Mexico in 1835; in 1838 it became a republic with the Freemason Sam Houston as President. May 11, 1838, Houston installed Anson Jones as Grand Master of Masons in Texas.

260. Wasn't a Freemason elected President of the United States in 1828, at the height of the anti-Masonic period?

"Old Hickory" in the person of Andrew Jackson, a Freemason who refused to renounce his membership, was overwhelmingly elected President in 1828. He was sworn in by another well-known Freemason, John Marshall, Chief Justice of the United States Supreme Court.

261. What important cornerstone did the Grand Lodge of Maryland lay in 1828?

Along with the participation of the Grand Masters from Virginia and Pennsylvania the Grand Master of Maryland presided at the laying of the cornerstone for the Baltimore and Ohio Railroad on July 4, 1828 in Baltimore.

262. What Freemason opposed the Mason Andrew Jackson for the Presidency in 1832?

Henry Clay. Jackson received 217 electoral votes; Clay, 49.

263. When and why did Henry Clay introduce one of his first compromises to ease friction among the states in the Senate?

South Carolina didn't like the tariffs on goods manufactured in the North that were supported by the Congress. It said it would refuse to collect them, and if force was used it would secede. President Jackson said any state that seceded would be guilty of treason, and he sent the Freemason, General Winfield Scott, to take command of the federal forces in the South. No other state joined South Carolina in 1832. Henry Clay introduced a resolution calling for a gradual reduction in the tariffs, the first of his several compromises to follow in an attempt to prevent a civil war.

264. Through what battle was a dispensation for a Lodge carried?

The Battle of Jacinto that brought independence from Mexico for Texas. In March, 1835, a group of Freemasons met in Texas and determined to ask the Grand Lodge of Louisiana for a dispensation to form Holland Lodge. The dispensation was handed to Anson Jones, who would become the first Grand Master in Texas, just before the battle, whose forces were under the command of Sam Houston, a Freemason. It is claimed at least 151 Freemasons were involved in this battle.

265. Were there Freemasons in the mission called "the Alamo" when it fell to Mexican forces?

Colonel William B. Travis, a Freemason, was in command of a force of less than 200 that was under siege for weeks before those still alive were annihilated by Santa Anna's superior forces. Among the known Masons were John C. Clarke, Alharon Dickenson, James Bonham and James Bowie.

266. Who were the Freemasons who were officials in the Republic of Texas?

Each of the Presidents and Vice Presidents were Freemasons: Houston, Mirabeau B. Lamar, David G. Burnet, Edward Burleson, Anson Jones, and Kenneth L. Anderson. Other officials were predominantly Freemasons. In 1845 Texas became a state.

8. Freemasonry Moves Forward

The venerable Institution of Masonry was planned in wisdom, and established on the firm and unshaken foundations of LOVE and FRIENDSHIP, in ages long since rolled away.... It has withstood the shocks of time, the revolutions of ages, the concussion of empires, and the convulsions of hostile contending nations.... The lightenings of vengeance have shot their fires of death, and the rolling thunders of human wrath and indignation have been heard in reverberating peals. The storm has spent its violence. The enemies in despair have retired from the field of conflict.
-From a letter written in 1839 and read
at the conclusion of 1843 Convention.-

267. How many Grand Lodges were formed between 1838 and 1851?

Seven. They were Arkansas where officers were elected on November 27, 1838; Illinois in 1840; Wisconsin on December 18, 1843; Iowa adopted a constitution on January 2, 1844 and on the 8th a Grand Master was installed; Michigan formed a Grand Lodge in 1829 with Lewis Cass, a Past Grand Master of Ohio, as its first Grand Master, then went out of existence, but it was revived in 1841, then on December 17, 1844 it was reorganized; California came into being on April 19, 1848; Oregon adopted a constitution and elected a Grand Master on September 15, 1851.

268. What problem did Illinois encounter soon after its Grand Lodge was formed?

Masons among the followers of the Mormon leader, Joseph Smith, petitioned the Grand Lodge for a dispensation to form a Lodge at Nauvoo. It was granted on March 15, 1842. Because it "made" 256 men members its dispensation was suspended six months later.

Brigham Young and his followers carried bitter memories of Masonry into Utah. There were many who believed the leaders of the Church of Latter Day Saints were not anti-Masonic, but the Grand Lodge of Utah banned Mormons until 1984. None of the other Grand Lodges, however, ever had any prohibition against that denomination.

269. When did Freemasonry first enter Wisconsin?

In 1824 a Lodge was established, chartered by the Grand Lodge of New York.

270. Where was the first Masonic library founded?

Soon after the Grand Lodge of Iowa was established in 1844, Theodore S. Parvin, with five dollars granted by the Grand Lodge, started a Masonic library now worth millions of dollars (if a price could be placed on its contents). Later it erected the first building anywhere in the world exclusively for use as a Masonic library. Today, in Cedar Rapids, it has a beautiful office and library building.

271. Who were some of the best known Freemasons to come from Iowa?

Among the many were Joseph Fort Newton, D.D., a world-renowned Christian minister, who wrote *The Builders*, perhaps the best selling Masonic book of all time; George Schoonover, who founded *The Builder*, a highly successful Masonic periodical, and "the father of The Masonic Service Association" (he was later suspended, but evidence indicates this was unwarranted); Charles C. Hunt, a highly respected Masonic writer; Harry Leroy Haywood, a Masonic author without peer in his day; Jacob Hugo Tatsch, author of *Freemasonry in the Thirteen Colonies*, many other books and Masonic articles, an officer in special services during World War II, a supporter of The Masonic Service Association, a vice president of Macoy Publishing and Masonic Supply Co. in New York; and more recently Jerald E. "Jerry" Marsengill, writer, author and long time editor of *The Philalethes* and *Royal Arch Mason* magazines.

272. Did any woman who supported Freemasonry come from the Masonic library in Iowa?

Miss Vee Hansen, a young girl who had been Tatsch's secretary, accepted his invitation to join him at Macoy's after he was established with the company in New York. This resulted in a windfall for Freemasonry. When the owners of the company died within months of each other, she was permitted to take over the company in 1945. She saved it from bankruptcy, later moved it to Richmond, Virginia, and built it into a prosperous company. It became the largest publisher of Masonic books and regalia in the country.

273. Was the Grand Lodge of Michigan recognized by other Grand Lodges when it was revived in 1841?

No. And one of its bitterest opponents was the Grand Lodge of New York, yet the reason for this opposition was never stated. In fact, the participants in the "Baltimore Convention" of 1843 refused to permit the delegates from Michigan to be seated.

274. Did Freemasonry in Michigan completely fade away along with its Grand Lodge?

No. (Actually, Freemasonry never totally dies anywhere it was once established.) The tiler of Stoney Creek Lodge placed a lighted candle in a window of his Lodge on every stated meeting night. He continued this until his Grand Lodge was once again established.

275. What was the Baltimore Convention?

It was "The Convention that Changed the Face of Freemasonry." It took place in Baltimore (thus the name) in May, 1843. It was first considered in 1839 when the Grand Lodge of Alabama requested all Grand Lodges to send a delegate to Washington, D.C., in March, 1842. It wanted a uniform of ritualistic work, and changes in regulations for the security of the Craft. This would strongly indicate the recent anti-Masonic furor had caused at least some of the Masonic leadership to worry about such future episodes. Only ten Grand Lodges were represented on March 7, 1842. The delegates decided not enough Grand Lodges were represented, so they voted to ask for a convention be held the following year.

276. Did the 1842 meeting in the District of Columbia have any influence on Freemasonry?

It certainly did! In spite of its sparse representation a committee made several suggestions that were quickly adopted by many Grand Lodges. Among these were: A Grand Lodge representative system be adopted by all Grand Lodges (this was then in its infancy); All Freemasons carry "certificates of good standing" to prevent impostors from attending Lodges; Payment for conferring degrees, instead of promissory notes, be demanded; All business should be conducted in the Master Mason degree. In less than a decade all United States Grand Lodges adopted this "suggestion." An Entered Apprentice was no longer considered entitled to "the franchise of members."

277. Didn't what has come to be known as "The Baltimore Convention" have a formal name?

Formally it was called a "National Masonic Convention."

278. When was this Convention held?

From May 8 to 17, 1843. It met in the Masonic Hall on Saint Paul Street in Baltimore, Maryland. Sixteen of the 23 Grand Lodges then in existence were represented.

279. Who was elected to preside over this Convention? What did he state its purpose to be?

John Dove, the Grand Secretary of the Grand Lodge of Virginia, was elected President of the Convention. In his opening remarks on the evening of May 8 Dove said: "For the first time in the Masonic history of the United States of North America, the Craft have found it necessary and expedient to assemble by their representatives, to **take into consideration the propriety of devising some uniform mode of action by which the ancient landmarks of our beloved Order may be preserved and perpetuated**, and by which posterity in all times to come may be enabled to decide with certainty upon the pretensions of a Brother, no matter in which section of our blessed and happy land he may reside; and, finally, and we hope no distant date, to transfer those inestimable privileges to our Brothers throughout the Masonic World." (Emphasis has been added because there are still many who believe this Convention was called only for the purpose of devising a uniform ritual for all Grand Lodges; nothing is further from the truth.)

280. What did the Committee on the General Object of the Convention report?

"The objects of the Convention are two-fold, viz: I. To produce uniformity of Masonic Work; II. To recommend such measures as shall tend to the elevation of the Order to its due degree of respect throughout the world at large." Another indication that the recent anti-Masonic fury was a deep concern.

281. What committees were set to work?

1. On work and lectures in conferring degrees; 2. On the funeral service; 3. On the ceremonies of Consecration and Installation; 4. On Masonic Jurisprudence.

282. Who were the members of the committee on ritual?

There were five. Three of them were probably the best ritualists of their day: John Dove of Virginia; John Barney (originally from Vermont) represented Ohio; and Charles W. Moore of Massachusetts. S.W.B. Carnegy represented Missouri, and Ebenezer Wadsworth of New York. For some unexplained reason, Wadsworth, on the second day, cast the only negative vote on the work of the committee after it recited the ritual of the first degree. Its rendition was accepted by the Convention, and Wadsworth asked to be excused from further participation on the committee. He was replaced by Edward Herndon of Alabama.

283. How did the Convention greet the remainder of the work of the committee on ritual?

After minor amendments, the Convention accepted the ritual of all the degrees and installation ceremony as enacted by the committee.

284. Did the Convention agree that a periodical devoted be established and published?

It did, and Charles Moore of Massachusetts was suggested as the man to publish such a periodical.

285. What did the Convention say about sojourning Masons?

It considered those who continually visited "foreign" Lodges as "free-loaders." It strongly suggested Grand Lodges adopt regulations requiring these visitors be required to "contribute a sum equal in value to the annual dues per capita of the subordinate Lodge in whose jurisdiction they reside."

286. Did the Convention believe there was unity within Freemasonry?

It was critical of the lack of unity. It concluded this was an evil that existed. Inter-communication between Grand Lodges rarely, if ever, took place.

287. What recommendation did the Convention suggest to cure the "evil" of the lack of unity?

It considered two plans at length: A General Grand Lodge; and a triennial convention of representatives of the several Grand Lodges. It discounted the General Grand Lodge proposition (in later years many believed this was recommended; but to repeat -- a General Grand Lodge was NOT considered prudent). The Convention strongly advised that the Grand Lodges send representatives to meet in a Masonic convention every three years.

288. Did the Grand Lodges accept the recommendation to meet nationally?

Not until 1925! It took The Masonic Service Association to show the Grand Lodges of the United States that the leadership of the Grand Lodges could meet and still control their sovereignty. (More on this later.)

289. Was a date set for another national Masonic Convention?

It was, for three years later. But it was never held, and there would be none until a special convention was held in 1918 for a completely different purpose. (See previous answer.)

290. What did the Convention say about Thomas Smith Webb?

"That the forms in the 'Monitor' under the authorship of M.W. Thomas S. Webb, republished in 1813, possesses the least faults of any which have been before them, and has a high claim to antiquity, and having been in general use as a standard work for nearly half a century, possess no errors of material as to require alteration, except as follows:" and there followed six minor changes.

291. Did all United States Grand Lodges adopt the Webb work as recommended by the Baltimore Convention?

Not exactly. Every Grand Lodge has differences in its ritualistic work. Even West Virginia, whose original Lodges were chartered by Virginia (and whose Grand Lecturer taught its Lodges the ritual after the Grand Lodge of West Virginia was founded), has several differences. What is considered secret in one jurisdiction may be written in another.

292. When did Freemasonry enter California?

No one really knows. There may have been active Freemasons there when James W. Marshall discovered gold at Sutter's Mill in January, 1848. When the word was spread, the population of San Francisco jumped from 900 to 20,000 within a year. On May 10, 1848 a charter from Missouri for Western Star Lodge No.98 was carried into California. But it was October 30, 1849 before the Lodge was organized at Lassen Trading Post.

293. Who presided over the Convention that established the Grand Lodge of California?

Charles Gilman, a Past Grand Master of Masons in New Hampshire and again in Maryland. Interestingly, the Convention was held in a building where the second floor was occupied by "participants in the world's oldest profession." On the seventy-fifth anniversary of the Concord incident that started the Revolutionary War, April 15, 1775, the Grand Lodge of California was formed.

294. How long did it take for a request for a dispensation to form a Lodge in Oregon to be received?

A request for a dispensation was agreed to on February 21, 1846. It was carried overland to Missouri. The request was granted on October 17, 1846, but it wasn't received on September 11, 1848! Why? It wasn't until April, 1848 that a wagon train left St. Joseph, Missouri, for Oregon. Hostile Indians held up this train until it was joined by a larger one from Ohio. Later the bearer of the dispensation left the train to join the gold seekers in California! He turned the document over to another who finally handed it to the petitioners in Oregon. On September 15, 1851 a Grand Lodge was formed.

295. When did what is now known as "Prince Hall Masonry" come into being?

On March 6, 1775 a sergeant named John Batt of the 38th Foot initiated one Prince Hall and 14 other black men as Masons. A short time later this British regiment left Boston, and Hall was given a permit to meet as a Lodge. This Lodge, African No. 1, requested a warrant from the Grand Lodge of England (Moderns). On September 28, 1784 the warrant was granted and African Lodge became No. 459 on the English roster.

296. Is Prince Hall Masonry "legitimate"?

Many consider it legitimate; others don't. In 1898 the Grand Lodge of Washington (state) adopted a resolution recognizing Prince Hall Masonry. The resulting condemnation of this resolution caused it to be later rescinded. In 1947, under the leadership of Melvin Maynard Johnson, the Grand Lodge of Massachusetts adopted a favorable report for Prince Hall Masonry. It was rescinded the following year. In 1989 the Grand Lodge of Connecticut recognized Prince Hall Masonry. Washington (state) and several others followed. Other Grand Lodges are studying the issue, but there has been little condemnation of those who have recognized the Masonry that has descended from the Lodge that received a charter from the Grand Lodge of England in 1784. It's interesting to note that the Grand Secretary of a Southern Grand Lodge, John Dove of Virginia, aided Prince Hall Masons following the American Civil War. He gave them his *Monitor* to use, and, slightly revised, it's followed to the present day.

9. The Undivided Craft

My father had been a soldier in the Southern army.... He was made a Mason in a military Lodge.... Taken prisoner at Arkansas Post, he was carried up the Mississippi River to Rock Island, Illinois.... My father became ... desperately ill, and made himself known as a Mason to an officer of the camp. The officer took him to his own home and nursed him back to life. When the war ended, he loaned Father money to pay his way back to his Texas home, and gave him a pearl-handled pistol to protect himself.... This experience of my father, when I learned about it, had a very great influence upon my life...; the fact that such a fraternity of men could exist, mitigating the harshness of war, and remain unbroken when states and churches were torn in two, became a wonder; and it is not strange that I tried for years to repay my debt to it.
                                                        -Joseph Fort Newton, D.D.
                                                        in *River of Years*-

297. Who was the President of the United States who participated at the laying of the cornerstone of the equestrian statue of George Washington in Richmond, Virginia?

    It was Zachary Taylor. The Grand Lodge of Virginia officiated at the cornerstone ceremony on February 22, 1850.

298. Was Zachary Taylor a Freemason?

    While he was President he said he wasn't because circumstances didn't permit him to be. He added: "I would do so now, but have got to be too old."

299. What did Taylor propose when California was about to be admitted to the Union?

He asked that California come into the Union as a free state, but that other territories be admitted with no reference to slavery.

300. Who was the Freemason who agreed with Taylor?

Senator Henry Clay of Kentucky in 1850 at the age of 72. He had been among the leaders of the "compromisers" who had kept the radicals of both sides partially satisfied for many years. (He was bitterly opposed by Senator John C. Calhoun of South Carolina.) He believed the South had given its opponents enough, and he pleaded for no more compromises. On March 4, 1850 his speech had to be read by someone else (he died a month later). Clay's compromises were finally adopted.

301. When was the cornerstone laid for the extension of the Capitol?

It was laid by the Grand Lodge of the District of Columbia on July 4, 1851. Millard Fillmore, who had succeeded to the Presidency on the death of Taylor, was a participant, although not a Freemason.

302. Who wrote the fictional story *Uncle Tom's Cabin*, or *Life Among the Lowly*?

Harriet Beecher Stowe. It first appeared in a magazine; in 1852 it was published as a book. It is claimed she had no firsthand knowledge of her subject. Several years later she was introduced to President Lincoln who asked: "Is this the little woman who made this big war?" It was the war that tore all organizations apart, with the exception of Freemasonry.

303. When was the Grand Lodge of Minnesota organized?

On February 24, 1853.

304. Who were the Freemasons who opposed each other for the Democratic nomination for the Presidency in 1856?

Stephen A. Douglas, a member of Springfield Lodge No. 4 of Illinois, and James Buchanan, a Past Master of Lodge No. 43 of

Pennsylvania, and who had served as the first District Deputy Grand Master of the first district in 1823. Buchanan won the nomination.

305. Which President was present when a monument was dedicated to James Buchanan?

Buchanan died on June 3, 1861. A monument was dedicated to his memory in Chicago on September 6, 1866, and Andrew Johnson, a Freemason, was present.

306. Why was the formation of the Grand Lodge of Kansas an outstanding event?

Anti and pro slavery elements appeared to be evenly divided in Kansas. The rifles of the "free-soil" (anti-slavery) settlers were called "Beecher's Bibles." Those who attended the various rallies went well-armed. It spoke well of the tolerance of Freemasons that an independent Grand Lodge could be formed under such circumstances. But it was, after three attempts, on March 17, 1856.

307. Was the abolitionist, John Brown, a Freemason?

Yes and no. He was made a Master Mason in Hudson Lodge No. 68, Ohio, on May 11, 1824. He moved to Pennsylvania in 1826, and with the anti-Masonic outbreak he, along with thousands of others, renounced Freemasonry. Perhaps his "soul went marching on" after his ill-fated raid on the United States arsenal at Harper's Ferry, which was in Virginia in 1859.

308. Who was John W. Geary, and for what Masonic gesture is he remembered?

Geary was made a Mason at Sight on January 4, 1847 in Pennsylvania, just before he left with his troops for Mexico (he then affiliated with Philanthropy Lodge No. 235 in Greensburg). When the bloody events in Kansas got out of hand, Geary was sent to the territory to take over as governor. Within weeks he had the situation under control. Later, at the fall of Savannah, Georgia, he was the commanding general. He placed Federal troops about the quarters of Solomon's Lodge No. 1 to save it from looting and damage. Later, while Geary was governor of Pennsylvania, the Lodge sent him a resolution of thanks. He answered by claiming it was the principles and tenets of Freemasonry that helped reconstruction to be as successful as it turned out to be. Within his reply he said: "... I feel again justified in referring to our beloved institution, by saying that to Freemasonry the people of the country are indebted for many mitigations of the suffering caused by the direful passions of war."

309. What was unusual about the formation of the Grand Lodge of Nebraska?

The three chartered Lodges were weak; there was no railroad within a hundred miles, or a telegraph line anywhere near these widely separated Lodges. Hostile Indians roamed all over the barren plains. And yet these three isolated Lodges joined together and formed a Grand Lodge on September 23, 1857.

310. When was the Grand Lodge of Washington formed?

Four Lodges, chartered by the Grand Lodge of Oregon, formed the Grand Lodge of Washington on December 8, 1858.

311. Where did President James Buchanan plead for all peoples in the United States to unite in friendship?

The President joined the Grand Lodge of the District of Columbia for the dedication ceremonies of the equestrian statute of George Washington on the anniversary of his birth, February 22, 1860. As the principal speaker he made it clear that he was addressing every citizen of the country. "May the God of our fathers preserve the Constitution and the Union for ages yet to come," he said. "In a word, may they endure as long as the name of Washington shall be honored and cherished among the children of men. May Washington City, which he founded, continue throughout many generations to be the seat of government of a great, peaceful, prosperous and united Confederacy."

312. Who were the Freemasons opposing Abraham Lincoln in the Presidential election of 1860?

Stephen Douglas of Illinois, John Bell of Tennessee and John C. Breckinridge of Kentucky. Without a single Southern vote, the Republican, Abraham Lincoln, won the election.

313. Which Freemason took over Henry Clay's position as a compromiser?

John J. Crittenden, a member of Lexington Lodge No. 1 of Kentucky, like his predecessor, didn't want to see the country torn asunder. The parcel of compromises that he submitted to the Senate was turned over to a committee. The Republicans on the committee, along with President Lincoln who said, "Let there be no compromise," killed the compromises, which even the New York *Tribune* considered conciliatory.

314. When was the Confederate States of America formed?

On February 18, 1861 in Montgomery, Alabama, and Jefferson Davis (not a Mason) was elected President. A little known fact is that, at the invitation of Virginia, 21 states met in Washington to try to keep the Union undivided. The only Northern state to agree to support Crittenden's compromises was New Jersey.

315. When it was learned Lincoln was sending supply ships to Fort Sumter at Charleston, South Carolina, who tried to prevent the order to fire on it?

Robert Toombs, a member of Lafayette Lodge No. 23 of Georgia, told President Davis: "The firing on that fort will inaugurate a civil war greater than any the world has yet seen... it is suicide, murder, and you will lose us every friend at the North." Jefferson Davis disagreed.

316. Who were the two principal Freemasons involved in the battle for Fort Sumter?

The Federal commander was Major Robert Anderson, a member of Mercer Lodge No.50 of New Jersey; the Confederate commander was General Pierre Gustave Toutant Beauregard, who had been one of Anderson's instructors at West Point. It should be noted that Beauregard was considered a Freemason and Knight Templar by many, including William R. Denslow who said so in his *10,000 Famous Freemasons*. Where and when he was made a Mason is not known.

317. Who became the first commander of Federal forces?

General Winfield Scott, a member of Dinwiddie Union Lodge No. 23 of Virginia. Scott was 75 years of age! Interestingly, Robert E. Lee (not a Mason) had turned down the offer of command.

318. Who succeeded Winfield Scott as commander of Federal forces?

After the Federal debacle at Bull Run, Lincoln fired Scott and appointed George B. McClellan, a member of Willamette Lodge No. 2 of Oregon.

319. Which Grand Lodge was organized during the early days of the Civil War?

A Grand Lodge was formed in Colorado on August 2, 1861.

320. What first informal meeting was held in the Territory of Colorado?

Seven Freemasons, claiming they were tired of being too long associated with "adventurers of dubious background, met in the settlement of Auraria, at the junction of Cherry Creek and the Platte. This became the first meeting of Masons in the Territory.

321. Where did the Reverend John M. Chivington preach his first sermon in Colorado?

In a Masonic Lodge in Denver shortly after his arrival on May 8, 1860. He wrote: "Henry Allen founded a Masonic Lodge in Colorado long before there was a church or school."

322. When was the first Masonic building erected in Colorado?

It was built in 1859 at Gregory Gulch, 40 miles northwest of Auraria in the high Rocky Mountains. About 100 Freemasons leveled the ground with ox teams dragging in logs for the hall. Four "tilers" with rifles and revolvers stood guard for the meetings. Over 200 names were entered on the rolls as visitors!

323. Who was the known Freemason who was among the Northerners who attempted to capture on April 12, 1862 the train called the "General" in Georgia?

Marion A. Ross. After he was captured and placed in a Chattanooga jail, several local Masons visited him. He was given money and other necessities which he shared with his fellow prisoners. Later Ross and seven other raiders were executed as spies. Other raiders were later exchanged.

324. Who was the Federal Freemason who was unpopular in New Orleans? Why?

He was Benjamin F. Butler of Massachusetts. Shortly after his arrival in New Orleans in April 1862 he ordered a desecrator of the American flag to be hanged with over a thousand spectators watching in horror. Later he earned the term of "Beast" when he issued an order calling any woman a prostitute who "insulted" a Federal soldier or officer "by gesture or movement."

325. What did the Freemason, Admiral David G. Farragut, tell the Mason Winfield Scott Schley, Captain of the gunboat *Winona* after a battle on the Mississippi River?

Farragut had ordered Schley to cease firing, but was ignored. The Admiral ordered the young man to board his ship. He publicly reprimanded Schley, then ordered him into his cabin. There he opened a bottle of sherry, produced and filled two glasses. Then he said: "Young man, if I commanded a gunboat and got into a mixup with the enemy, and was getting the better of him, I'll be damned if I'd see a signal either!"

326. Why was the Freemason McClellan not successful in capturing Richmond in early 1862?

There were many reasons, but it was principally because President Lincoln called the forces of McDowell back to Washington, thereby preventing them from reinforcing McClellan as had been planned. Lee had sent "Stonewall" Jackson (not a Mason) to appear to threaten the Federal capital. (See Preface.)

327. During the Seven Days Battle in May-June 1862 that covered territory from Mechanicsville to Harrison's Landing close to Richmond, how were McClellan's forces able to escape?

The escape was made possible by the troops of the 5th New Hampshire Regiment, commanded by the Freemason, Colonel Edward E. Cross, a member of North Star Lodge No. 8 of New Hampshire. Federal engineers had built bridges over the Chickahominy River, but the flood, caused by heavy rains during the latter days of May and early June, washed away those bridges. Only "Grapevine Bridge" built by Cross's men from May 28 - 30 survived the raging water. It was the only escape route left for the Federal troops.

328. Did the 5th New Hampshire Regiment have a traveling Military Lodge?

It did. The Grand Lodge of New Hampshire issued the Freemasons in the Regiment a warrant designating it as Hughes' Army Lodge. The commanding officer, Colonel Edward E. Hughes was among its members. The names of its petitioners, and many of its members and candidates, can be found in the office of the Grand Lodge of New Hampshire.

329. Which Confederate General who was a Freemason played havoc with superior Federal forces in the South?

Nathan Bedford Forrest of Angerona Lodge No. 168 of Tennessee. He was unschooled, but a brilliant military tactician. After the war he helped form the Ku Klux Klan to help protect Southerners from unscrupulous Northern "carpetbaggers." When scalawags took control of the KKK, Forrest ordered it disbanded, but those then in control ignored him. He completely relinquished his connections with this group.

330. Who was the Freemason generally credited with winning the Battle of Antietam?

General George B. McClellan of Oregon. He had been unjustly fired by Abraham Lincoln for failing to take Richmond in the spring of 1862. When Robert E. Lee's troops marched into Maryland in September 1862 the Federals were virtually leaderless. At Antietam Creek, near Sharpsburg, Maryland, McClellan was called on to stop the Confederates. On September 17 over 23,000 men were killed or wounded, the bloodiest single day of fighting ever. Lee's forces finally had to retreat.

331. Were there any Masonic episodes worthy of perpetuating during or after the Battle at Antietam?

Many. One involved the 5th New Hampshire. On the morning following the battle, Confederate sharpshooters fired at anything that moved. A wounded Confederate handed a Federal picket a piece of cloth on which a symbol was crudely drawn in blood. The picket carried it to a captain who recognized it as a Masonic emblem. The captain told Colonel Cross a wounded Confederate needed help. Cross asked for volunteers and several Masons offered to help. At the risk of their lives they went to and carried Lieutenant Edon of the Alabama Volunteers to the 5th New Hampshire hospital. Edon told them about another Mason lying wounded in the corn field. Back they went and carried him to join the other enemy soldier. Both received the same treatment as did the Federal wounded from the surgeon, a Freemason, William Child.

332. What future President of the United States gained fame during the Battle of Antietam?

Sergeant (later Major) William McKinley of Ohio became the first man of any commissary department to provide a hot meal for troops on the front lines during any battle. At the close of the war, on May 1, 2, and 3, 1865 in Winchester Hiram Lodge in Virginia, McKinley received the three degrees of Freemasonry.

333. Didn't Rob Morris, a Past Grand Master of Masons in Mississippi, form an organization that was intended to bring Freemasonry under his control?

Many Grand Lodges thought so and did "outlaw" Morris' "Conservators of Symbolic Masonry." He set himself up as the "Chief Conservator." He published a book of mnemonics (a cipher or code of his version of the Masonic ritual) and attempted to make this universal. He found defenders in several Grand Lodges, but the list of his members was never revealed. It has been estimated that he did have about 3,500 followers. His detractors were overwhelming, however. What influence the Conservators gained during its life of five years ended on June 24, 1865.

334. During the war, wasn't Freemasonry blamed for the draft?

It was in several places, but the reason for placing this blame on Freemasonry was never made clear. An example occurred in Wisconsin where the Lodge hall in Port Washington was wrecked on November 10, 1862 by a mob that blamed Masonry for the draft.

335. What proof is there that Freemasonry remained a "House Undivided" during the Civil War?

The proof is abundant. An episode took place in Galveston, Texas, on January 2, 1863. Captain I.W. Wainwright of the *U.S.S. Harriet Lane* was killed. Several of his men, prisoners of war, vouched for Wainwright's Masonic affiliation. Harmony Lodge No. 6 was opened for the purpose of conducting the funeral for Wainwright. The Master of this Lodge was P.C. Tucker, a Confederate Major on the staff of General Magruder. A public procession consisting of "both friends and foe wearing the insignia of the Order, and accompanied with a proper military escort" accompanied the body to the Episcopal Cemetery. There a Masonic funeral was conducted.

336. Wasn't another Federal naval officer buried by Confederate Masons?

The Federal gunboat *U.S.S. Albatross,* under the command of John Hart hurled shell after shell into the village of St. Francisville, Louisiana. Later a small boat under a flag of truce tied up at a wharf. The executive officer asked for a Mason. The Senior Warden of Feliciana Lodge No. 31, W.W. Leake, answered the call. When informed that Captain Hart, who was a Freemason, was dead, Leake immediately offered to open his Lodge and bury Hart with Masonic rites. Over the years the United Daughters of the Confederacy kept his grave fresh and green. In 1972 the Grand Lodge of Louisiana replaced the simple headstone with a monument that covered Hart's entire grave. It said: "This monument is dedicated in loving tribute to the universality of Freemasonry."

337. Who was the Freemason who saw the first action in what would become the Battle of Gettysburg?

Confederate General Henry Heth, the last Senior Warden of Rocky Mountain Lodge No. 205 in Utah. He pushed the Federal troops through the streets of Gettysburg until they were rallied on the heights near Cemetery Ridge by the Federal General Winfield S. Hancock, a member of Charity Lodge No. 190 of Pennsylvania.

338. What was the episode that occurred during the Battle of Gettysburg that would be commemorated in 1993 by the Grand Lodge of Pennsylvania?

Thousands of Confederates stormed the hills on which the Federal forces were dug in. Among the Confederates leading the charge on July 3, 1863 were Generals George E. Pickett, a member of Petersburg Lodge No. 15, James L. Kemper of Linn Banks Lodge No. 126, and Lewis A. Armistead of Alexandria Washington Lodge No. 22, all of Virginia. The latter was mortally wounded when he reached the top of the ridge. Federal Colonel (later General) Henry H. Bingham was sent by General Hancock to assist their Masonic Brother. This act became a monument commissioned and donated by the Grand Lodge of Pennsylvania. It was unveiled on August 21, 1993 at the National Cemetery Annex at Gettysburg. Its inscription says: "Friend to Friend—A Brotherhood Undivided."

339. Northern and Southern sympathizers caused a Lodge in Colorado to take an unusual action. What was it?

In Denver Lodge No. 5 the members appeared to be evenly divided in their affinity for the opposing sides in the war. This appeared to be a problem that couldn't be overcome, so the Lodge recommended to the Grand Lodge that a charter be granted for the formation of Union Lodge. It was granted. But not a single member of Denver Lodge demitted to affiliate with the new one! They had learned it is not necessary for all Freemasons to think alike to remain friends and Brothers.

340. What happened to the Masonic building in Vicksburg, Mississippi, during and after the siege of that area?

It remained undamaged, although it was a prominent edifice. It was used as a Confederate hospital, and after the fall of Vicksburg on July 4, 1863, Federal forces used it for the same purpose.

341. What event concerning Freemasonry occurred in Chambersburg, Pennsylvania?

General Lee sent General John C. Breckinridge, a Freemason, to raid the Federal capital. Due to the reinforcements provided by another Mason, General Lew Wallace (of *Ben Hur* fame), the invasion was foiled. However, during the Confederate retreat, Chambersburg was torched on July 30, 1864, but the Masons among the Confederates made certain the Masonic building was left undamaged.

342. What happened to the oldest Masonic building in the country when Richmond, Virginia, fell to Federal forces on April 2-3, 1865?

Mobs burned warehouses, blew up ships, and generally set fire to the property along the James River. Masons' Hall, built in 1785 and which was the first permanent home of the Grand Lodge of Virginia, was close to this area. The Federal Provost Marshal, A. H. Stevens, a member of Putnam Lodge in Massachusetts, placed a guard about the building, plus the homes of several members of the Lodge. Shortly thereafter, Federal and Confederate members of the Craft met in harmony in the same building.

343. Who was the Freemason that Grant left at Appomattox, Virginia, to accept the surrender of Confederate forces?

On Sunday, April 9, 1865 General Lee agreed to the terms of surrender set by General Grant. General Joshua L. Chamberlain of United Lodge No. 8 of Maine was Grant's excellent choice to accept the surrender. Three days later the Confederate Army of Northern Virginia, led by the Old Stonewall Brigade, sorrowfully stacked their arms. Much of their bitterness left when Chamberlain ordered his troops to give their former enemy soldiers a full military salute!

344. Did the commander who surrendered Fort Sumter return?

He did. On April 14, 1865 (now) General Robert Anderson, the Freemason, aided by the Freemason Peter Hart, raised the same battle-scarred flag they had removed four years earlier.

345. What one act has been cited, perhaps, above most others to show brotherhood in action during the American Civil War?

On June 4, 1861, Thomas Hart Benton, Jr., Grand Master of Masons in Iowa, told his Grand Lodge of his sorrow with the events taking place in the political arena. He said he, among other Freemasons, had "labored, though feebly and ineffectually, to avert the awful crisis. It has been my good fortune to press the fraternal hand in various parts of our country, from New England to Texas, and from the Atlantic to the Missouri. This consideration alone were sufficient to enlist my undivided energies in word and deed to perpetuate the friendly relations once so common among us as a people." He proved his sincerity. As the General in command of Federal forces that occupied Little Rock, Arkansas, after the city was evacuated on September 10, 1863, he placed a Federal guard about the home of the Confederate General, Albert Pike, to save his valuable library.

10. Shambles and Shame

Let not politics be mentioned in your Lodges, and know no difference in men because of political or religious distinctions.... Masonry should take no part in civil strife, except to throw the broad mantle of Masonic charity over the faults of our brethren, succor the needy, and apply the oil of consolation and the wine of joy to the afflicted, especially of those of our own household.... Amid subsiding kingdom and crumbling empires, our Mystic Brotherhood still stands, the great beacon of life in ages, the friend of justice, the preserver of peace and humanity.
           J. D. Landrum, Grand Master of Masons in Kentucky
              (in answer to questions about Masonic attendance at Masonic funerals of those who fought for the Confederacy, and whether or not the widows and orphans of such Masons are entitled to Masonic charity.)

346. When and why was the first Masonic meeting held in Nevada?

The first meeting was held in Virginia City for the funeral of Captain Edward Faris Storey. He had been killed in a battle with the "Pah-Ute Indians" on June 2, 1860. The first Masonic Lodge was formed in Carson City to assist those traveling West. On February 27, 1862 Samuel L. (Mark Twain) Clemens's first visit to this Lodge was recorded. He was a member of Polar Star Lodge No. 99 of Missouri, and he was a reporter for the *Territorial Enterprise* of Virginia City.

347. Why did William McKinley determine to become a Freemason?

While accompanying a doctor attending wounded Confederates he noted the surgeon treating many of them especially kindly, and giving some of them money. When McKinley asked him why, he said they were Brother Masons. McKinley asked him how he could become one. Soon he was given a petition for Winchester Hiram Lodge No. 21. He received the three degrees on May 1, 2, 3, 1865.

348. Masonic Lodges were draped in mourning after the assassination of President Abraham Lincoln. Was he a Freemason?

Lincoln was not a Freemason; however, thousands of Masons highly respected him for varying reasons. Incidentally, Edwin Booth, a member of New York Lodge No. 350, was the brother of John Wilkes Booth. Edwin told his Lodge that the crime had crushed him, and he abhorred the act.

349. Did the Grand Lodge of Virginia approve the formation of the Grand Lodge of West Virginia?

Not for several years. There was resentment in many circles at the manner in which the state was formed. (And to this day there are those who believe it was illegally declared a separate entity.) All of the Lodges in West Virginia were chartered by the Grand Lodge of Virginia. On June 24, 1864 officers in West Virginia were elected, but they refused to be installed. On April 12, 1865 another full slate of officers was elected; these were installed on May 10, 1865. It was December 16, 1868 when the Grand Lodge of Virginia approved this formation—and the older Grand Lodge permitted the Lodges in its sister jurisdiction to retain their Virginia charters!

350. Who succeeded Lincoln as President of the United States?

Andrew Johnson, who had become a member of Greeneville Lodge No. 119 of Tennessee in 1851.

351. How did the new President feel about the welfare of the people in the former Confederate States of America?

He evidently believed in the Masonic principles of Brotherly Love and charity. He said of the Congress: "Before our brave men have scarcely returned to their homes to renew the ties of affection and love, we find ourselves almost in the *midst of another rebellion.*" On Washington's birthday, February 22, 1866, he spoke again of what the politicians were doing: "... You denied in the beginning of the struggle that any State had the right to go out. You said that they had neither the right nor the power. The issue has been made, and it has been settled that a State has neither the right nor the power to go out of the Union. And when you have settled that by the executive and military power of the Government, and by the public judgment, *you turn around and assume that they are out and shall not come in."* He added: *"I will be found standing by the Constitution as the chief rock of our safety,* as the palladium of our civil and religious liberty."

352. Did the Freemasons of the country agree with President Johnson?

It appeared that they did. Freemasons from the North continued assisting their Brethren and their families in the South. They did this financially and in other ways.

353. Who led the fight to defeat President Johnson's orders to ease vindictive reconstruction rules against the former Confederate states?

The anti-Mason Thaddeus Stevens of Pennsylvania managed to have a special committee appointed to "study the whole question of reconstruction." He thereby kept those elected from the South from taking their seats in the Congress.

354. What action by the Congress led to a resolution of impeachment?

To prevent the President from firing those in his administration who were not in sympathy with his beneficial policies to the South, the Congress passed "the Tenure in Office Act." When Johnson fired his Secretary of War, Edwin M Stanton, a member of Steubenville Lodge No. 45 of Ohio, the "Radicals" pounced on this action. A resolution of impeachment was adopted on February 24, 1868.

355. Was President Johnson impeached by the House of Reprentatives?

Yes. But the President was acquitted in the Senate by one vote! The "trial" began on March 30, 1868. The first vote was taken on May 16. It stood at 35 guilty; 19 not guilty, one vote short of the most obnoxious act ever perpetrated by the Congress of the United States. The opponents took another vote ten days later. The vote was the same. The radicals quit. By one vote the Masonic principles of Andrew Johnson were upheld.

356. Is there a record of how the Senators voted in the impeachment trial?

There is. But here we are concerned with the actions of Freemasons. Fifteen Senators were Freemasons (plus one Entered Apprentice). Ten of these, plus the Entered Apprentice, voted for conviction; five, not guilty. Those voting guilty were: Richard Yates, Sr. (R), Harmony No. 3, Illinois; Zachariah Chandler (R), Detroit No. 2, Michigan; John Milton Thayer (R), Capitol No. 101 (now No. 3), Nebraska; William Morris Stewart (R), Nevada No. 13, Nevada; James Warren Nye (R), Hamilton No. 120, New York; Aaron Harrison Cragin (R), Franklin No. 6, New Hampshire; George Henry Williams (R), Harmony No. 12, Oregon; Simon Cameron (R), Past Master of Perseverance No. 21, Pennsylvania; William Sprague (R), St. John's No. 2, Rhode Island; George Franklin Edmunds (R), Washington No. 3, Vermont; and Oliver Hazard Perry Throckmorton (an EA), (R), Hiram Lodge No. 42 (now No. 417), Indiana. The five Freemasons voting against conviction were: James Dixon (R) St. John's No. 4, Connecticut; Willard Saulsbury, Sr. (D), Franklin No. 12, Delaware; Edmund Gibson Ross (R), Topeka No. 17, Kansas; Garrett Davis (D), Grand Orator, Grand Lodge of Kentucky; and William Pitt Fessenden (R), Rising Virtue No. 10, Maine.

357. What happened to Andrew Johnson after the impeachment trial?

He refused to be a candidate for election to the Presidency. He returned to Kentucky, where he was urged to run for the Senate. He was elected and returned to the District of Columbia in March, 1875. He attacked the corruption and unethical conduct of the Grant administration, and the public cheered. When the Congress adjourned he returned home. There he suffered two strokes, which resulted in his death on July 31, 1875. His family respected his wishes and called on the Fraternity he loved to make the arrangements for his funeral.

358. Other than Johnson's request for the Freemasons to officiate at his funeral, what other requests had he made?

"Pillow my head on the Constitution of my country," he had asked. The copy he had purchased in 1835, which was filled with notes and comments, provided that pillow. "Let the flag of the Nation be my winding sheet." It was, and his lifeless fingers grasped its folds.

359. Which Lodge conducted Johnson's funeral?

Greeneville No. 119, the Lodge of both Andrew Johnson and Andrew Jackson.

360. When was the Grand Lodge of Idaho organized?

On December 17, 1867. It was organized by Lodges that had received charters from Oregon and Washington.

361. When did Freemasonry appear in Utah?

In 1858. President James Buchanan, a Freemason, sent troops to the Territory because it was claimed that Brigham Young and his Mormon followers, some of whom were Masons, were defying the laws of the United States. Among the soldiers settling at Camp Floyd were several Masons. They asked the Grand Lodge of Missouri for a dispensation to form a Lodge. It was granted on March 6, 1859 and Rocky Mountain Lodge No. 205 was established.

362. What happened to Rocky Mountain Lodge No. 205?

In a single year it conferred 162 degrees! But the Secretary wrote: "Grand Lodge cannot boast of better material than this Lodge has engrafted upon our ancient and honorable institution."

363. Who was the first Master of the Lodge?

John C. Robinson, who would become a Federal Major General (see the following answer).

364. What was unusual about the Lodge's annual return on December 27, 1860?

It noted that the office of Senior Warden was vacant. Henry Heth had resigned this office to join the Confederacy. Heth became a colonel of Virginia infantry on June 17, 1861; a Brigadier General, January, 1862; Major General, May, 1863. He and his friend and Brother, the first Master of Rocky Mountain Lodge, met once again during the Battle of Gettysburg.

365. When was the Grand Lodge of Utah organized?

On January 18, 1872.

366. Does the Grand Lodge of Utah prohibit members of the Church of the Latter Day Saints (Mormons) from petitioning its Lodges?

It did at one time, but this was changed in 1984. Now there is no prohibition in either quarter.

367. Where was the first Masonic meeting in Wyoming held?

On a rock estimated to be two billion years old. Several wagon trains camped near Independence Rock on July 4, 1862. An altar was built with 13 stones (representing the original colonies). Jewels were cut out of cardboard. Twelve years later, on December 15, 1874, officers were installed to conclude the establishment of the Grand Lodge of Wyoming.

368. Which Grand Lodge issued the first dispensations and charters for Lodges in Dakota Territory?

Iowa. On April 23, 1862 it issued a dispensation for the formation of Dakotah Lodge at Fort Randall, but there is no evidence that this Lodge ever met. Iowa issued another Dispensation on December 2, 1862 for St. John's Lodge at Yankton. It issued others in 1869, in 1871, and in 1875. On June 22-24, 1875 a convention was held at Elk Point to form a Grand Lodge. On the 24th officers were elected. On July 21, in the Baptist Church at Vermillion, Dakota Territory, the officers were installed by T.S. Parvin of Iowa.

369. What was unusual about Freemasonry entering the Territory of New Mexico?

John Balls, Grand Master of Masons in Missouri, issued a dispensation for Missouri Military Lodge of the Third Regiment of Missouri Volunteers—an organization with which he was serving! He installed the officers of the Lodge. Then they marched 900 miles into Santa Fe. In September 1847 it received a charter, and held the first official Masonic meeting in an expanse that "is now occupied by thirteen separate Grand Lodges," claimed LaMoine Langston in 1977, a hundred fifty years later.

370. When was a Grand Lodge formed in New Mexico?

On August 7, 1877 a constitution was adopted and Grand Lodge officers elected. The Governor of the Territory, Samuel B. Antell, was the Master of Ceremonies; Thomas B. Catron, who would become New Mexico's first United States Senator, was appointed Grand Lecturer. The West was on the way to being won.

11. Westward

The Canal Zone was transformed from a pest hole to a healthy and attractive place for human habitation. Without the splendid work of the Medical Department, it is doubtful that George W. Goethals would have had the success he did. Today, the canal stands as a lasting monument to the technical ability, discipline and efficiency of the Army working at its best in the fulfillment of a peacetime mission. Its completion partially freed the Nation of the heavy cost of maintaining an enormous fleet in both the Atlantic and Pacific since it permitted vessels to move quickly to any point of need in either ocean.
-American Military History-

371. How did those traveling westward, and those settling in where there was no formal law, protect themselves?

"Hemp Justice" (hanging) and pistols became a way of life. Vigilantes often protected settlements against the lawless. Many of these groups were composed of Masons.

372. What did those traveling westward in the 1870s have to endure?

The wife of James H. Peabody, a member of Mt. Moriah Lodge No. 15 of Carson City, who would later become governor of Colorado, recalled her impressions: The crack of the bullsnake whips, the creaking and jolting of the wagons, the straining, odor and sweat of the oxen, the clanking of the heavy chains used to keep the wheels from running over the oxen in steep places, the sandstorms, the rainstorms, the blizzards. But she considered her party lucky — it didn't have to fight off hostile Indians.

373. What helped make the trek westward easier?

The completion of the transcontinental railroad. It was started in 1866, in the west by the Central Pacific, in the east by the Union Pacific. Three years later the 1,775 miles of track met at Promontory Point, Utah.

374. Who drove the golden spike, the last spike, that linked the tracks of the intercontinental railroad?

Governor Leland Stanford of California, a member of Michigan City Lodge No. 47 of California. According to historians, a regimental band played, with workers, saloon keepers, gamblers, prostitutes, money lenders, cooks, dishwashers and many other characters looking on.

375. How was the news of the uniting of the tracks transmitted?

By a telegrapher, high on a pole. To San Francisco and New York he tapped out: "Stand by, we have done praying." With the news that the spike had been driven, a hundred guns were fired in New York, the Liberty Bell was rung in Philadelphia, "the annexation of the United States" was proclaimed in San Francisco.

376. Who were the Republican contenders for the Presidential nomination in 1880?

One faction wanted U.S. Grant returned; another faction, led by James A. Garfield, wanted John Sherman of Ohio. After 36 ballots Garfield was chosen as a compromise candidate.

377. Who was James A. Garfield?

Garfield became a Master Mason in Columbia Lodge No. 30 on November 22, 1864, at the request of Magnolia Lodge No. 20 of Columbus, Ohio. Within a year he affiliated with Garrettsville No. 246, close to Hiram College. In 1869 he became a charter member of Pentalpha Lodge No. 23 in the District of Columbia. In May 1861 he was a colonel in the Ohio Volunteers, later becoming a major general. In 1863 he became a congressman, and on March 4, 1881 he was inaugurated President of the United States, the last of "the log cabin Presidents."

378. How long did Garfield serve as President?

On July 2, 1881, less than four months after Garfield's inauguration, a disgruntled office seeker, Charles J. Guiteau, shot him. He died from his wounds on September 10.

379. How did the death of Garfield affect Virginia Freemasonry?

It didn't, but it could have. Through the influence of Garfield the Grand Lodge of Virginia was asked to lay the cornerstone of Victory Monument at Yorktown, and Garfield had accepted an invitation to be present. To the relief of the Masonic officials in Virginia, President Chester Alan Arthur, not a Freemason, agreed to participate.

380. When was the cornerstone of Victory Monument at Yorktown laid?

After apologizing for the primitive conditions at Yorktown on October 17, 1881, the cornerstone was laid with Masonic ceremonies by the Grand Lodge of Virginia. Grand Masters from all the original colonies, with the exception of Georgia, participated.

381. What did the Yorktown ceremony prove?

By requesting the Grand Lodge of the former capital of the Confederate States to perform the ceremony of laying the cornerstone at Yorktown, there was proof that Freemasonry was once again considered a valued champion of Brotherhood in the United States. The federal government, by recognizing this time-honored ceremony, had set aside the animosity of the anti-Masonic fiasco of the decade beginning in 1826, and the rupture caused by the American Civil War. The episode has more favorable implications than can be recorded in a short space.

382. When was the cornerstone of the Statue of Liberty laid?

On August 5, 1884 the Grand Lodge of New York laid the cornerstone on Bedloe's (now Liberty) Island in New York Harbor. It was laid in the pedestal of the "Statue of Liberty Enlightening the World."

383. Who designed the Statue of Liberty?

Frederic A. Bartholdi, a Frenchman who was a member of Lodge Alsace-Lorraine of Paris, France. The members of his lodge marched in a body on June 19, 1884 to review his masterpiece, which would be a gift from the French people to the United States.

384. During this period, who was helping the railroad passengers to travel in comfort?

George Pullman, a member of Renovation Lodge No. 97 of New York built the first sleeping car in 1863; he devised dining cars in 1868; chair cars in 1875; and vestibule cars in 1887.

385. When was the Grand Lodge of Arizona organized?

Aztlan Lodge at Prescott received a charter from California in 1866; in 1879 Arizona Lodge at Phoenix received a dispensation from California; White Mountain Lodge at Globe received one from New Mexico in 1880; Tucson Lodge received one, also in 1880, from California; in 1881 Solomon Lodge at Tombstone requested and received a dispensation from California. These Lodges met at Phoenix in 1882 to form the Grand Lodge of Arizona. Among those helping the Grand Lodge celebrate its 100th anniversary year were the Virginia Craftsmen.

386. Who were among the first Freemasons to travel in the Dakota Territory?

Meriwether Lewis, a member of Door to Virtue Lodge No. 44 of Virginia (later this lodge became dormant and most of its members transferred to Widow's Son No. 60 in Charlottesville), and William Clark, a member of St. Louis Lodge No.111, then under a Pennsylvania charter. In 1935 the Grand Lodge of North Dakota erected a monument on the site where their expedition spent the winter of 1804-05.

387. Why was the first Masonic ceremony conducted in North Dakota?

To conduct the funeral of Lieutenant Fred J. Holt Beaver, a soldier attached to the staff of General H. H. Sibley. Beaver was killed in a skirmish with hostile Indians. The Deputy Grand Master of Minnesota convened a Masonic Lodge and conducted a Masonic funeral service. A marker was placed at the site in 1920 at Apple Creek, near Bismarck, to commemorate this event.

388. Which Lodges in this region "lived" under three Grand Lodges?

Shiloh and Bismarck were subordinate to the Grand Lodges of Minnesota, Dakota and North Dakota.

389. When was Dakota divided?

It became North and South Dakota when they were admitted to the Union on November 2, 1889. On June 13, 1890 separate Grand Lodges came into being.

390. What did Harry Leroy Haywood say about Oklahoma?

"Oklahoma was found, founded, and settled by Indians, most of them belonging to civilized tribes: Cherokee, Chickasaw, Creek, and Seminole peoples. They largely came from Florida, Georgia, and Tennessee." He later added: "During these formative years, and through the dreadful war period, Arkansas mothered Indian Territory, not its Grand Lodge only, but its lodges, and even individual members."

391. Why is Oklahoma unique among Grand Lodges?

It was organized in 1874 as the Grand Lodge of Indian Territory; in 1892 it became the Grand Lodge of Oklahoma Territory; in 1909 these were united into the Grand Lodge of Oklahoma.

392. Who was William McKinley?

McKinley won the election for the Presidency in 1896. He had served valiantly with Ohio troops during the American Civil War. In May 1865 he received the degrees of Masonry in Winchester Hiram Lodge No. 21 in Virginia with Confederate and Federal troops in attendance.

393. Who was McKinley's opponent for the election to the Presidency?

Masonic Trivia (and Facts)

William Jennings Bryan was McKinley's democratic opponent. In 1902 Bryan became a Master Mason in Lincoln Lodge No. 19, Nebraska.

394. Was McKinley in favor of going to war to free Cuba from Spanish control?

No. McKinley worked to prevent war. But much of the press, led by Randolph Hearst, called the President "spineless," among the kinder terms.

395. What was the catalyst that brought about the war with Spain?

The mysterious blowing up of the *U.S.S. Maine* in Havana harbor on February 15, 1898. At least 260 Americans were killed in this disaster.

396. Who was Theodore Roosevelt?

He was the Assistant Secretary of the Navy in the McKinley administration, and he supported the faction that wanted to fight Spain. After giving orders to Commodore George Dewey to bottle up the Spanish fleet in Asiatic waters, left the navy to become a "Rough Rider." His horseless corps gained immortality by charging up San Juan Hill. After the Spaniards were quickly defeated, Roosevelt returned to his former job.

397. Who became the military governor of Cuba?

Leonard C. Wood, who had been the commander of the Rough Riders. He had received both medical and law degrees from Harvard. He had been awarded the Congressional Medal of Honor for his campaign against hostile Indians in 1886. He became a Master Mason in 1916 in Anglo Saxon Lodge No. 137, New York City.

398. Was McKinley a candidate for reelection to the Presidency?

Reluctantly he agreed to run for a second term, and he chose Theodore Roosevelt as his running mate.

399. Was Theodore Roosevelt a Freemason?

He received the Masonic degrees in Matinecock Lodge No. 806, Oyster Bay, New York, in 1901.

400. What happened to McKinley on September 6, 1901?

After his speech in the Temple of Music in Buffalo, New York, he was shot by Leon Czolgosz while shaking hands with well-wishers. He died Saturday morning, September 14. In Buffalo, Theodore Roosevelt was sworn in as President.

401. What was among Theodore Roosevelt's most notable accomplishments?

He pushed through the 50 plus year attempt to build the Panama Canal. Through a treaty the United States was granted exclusive control of the Canal Zone in perpetuity, along with other sites necessary for the defense of the Canal. This would remain in force until 1978 when the then President (James Earl "Jimmy" Carter) and the Congress, by one vote, agreed to give it away at the turn of the century. (See quote at beginning of this chapter.)

402. What did Roosevelt do to earn the Nobel Peace Prize?

He received it in 1906 for his efforts in bringing the leaders of the war between Japan and Russia to New Hampshire. There they signed a peace treaty.

403. Who did Roosevelt support for the Presidency in 1908?

William Howard Taft. He was elected. The following year he was Made a Mason at Sight by the Grand Master of Masons in Ohio. He was then elected to membership in Kilwinning Lodge No.356, the lodge in which his father and half-brother were members.

404. Was Taft active in Freemasonry?

He was. He participated in dozens of Masonic functions. At the George Washington Masonic National Memorial on November 1, 1923, while Chief Justice of the Supreme Court, he said: "Masonry aims at the promotion of morality and higher living by the cultivation of the social side of man, the rousing in him of the instincts of charity and the foundation of the brotherhood of man and the fatherhood of God."

12. War and Brotherhood

It is recorded in history that when the Constitutional Convention, which met in Philadelphia in 1787 adjourned, Benjamin Franklin, then a very old man, and a representative from the great state of Pennsylvania, arose and pointing to the chair in which George Washington sat and on which is delineated, or was at the time, a half sun, with the rays, said, 'Men of America, during the long days of this Convention I have been wondering whether that was a rising or a setting sun. I am convinced that it is a rising sun.'

-Walter Lincoln Stockwell, of Nebraska-
at the close of the formation of
The Masonic Service Association

405. Did Freemasonry have anything to do with World War I?

No — and yes! It wasn't involved in starting the war. Unbelievably, this conflict began with the assassination of a little-known Archduke Francis Ferdinand of Austria on June 28, 1914. The dispute that followed pitted old alliances against each other, and Europe went to war.

406. Did the United States remain neutral?

It did, for three years. President Woodrow Wilson (not a Freemason) even accepted apologies from the German government for the sinking by U-boats of United States vessels. Wilson's keeping the United States out of the war helped him win reelection in 1916.

407. What caused the United States to enter the conflict?

Wilson claimed Germany was attempting to form an alliance

with Mexico and Japan, and American shipping was continually being sunk by German U-boats. The President asked the Congress for a declaration of war. It was officially declared on April 6, 1917.

408. Was the country prepared to fight?

With the exception of the U.S. navy (thanks to Theodore Roosevelt's foresight), the country, as it always had been, was unprepared. Another Freemason, Sydney N. Baruch, had invented depth charges to do battle with submarines. U.S. destroyers were well armed with these when war was declared.

409. Who was made Commander-in-Chief of the American Expeditionary Force that would fight overseas?

General John J. "Black Jack" Pershing.

410. Who was John J. Pershing?

Pershing became a Master Mason in Lincoln Lodge No. 19 of Nebraska on December 22, 1888. He later was made an Honorary Member of several lodges and appendant bodies. On September 24, 1942 he was elected to honorary membership in the Grand Lodge of Missouri. Harry S. Truman, a Past Grand Master of Masons in Missouri, and then Senator, presented Pershing with the Grand Lodge certificate while he was a patient at Walter Reed Hospital. In 1906 another Mason, Theodore Roosevelt, had taken the unprecedented action of promoting Captain Pershing to Brigadier General! (While in the Philippines Roosevelt had noted his extraordinary leadership qualities.)

411. What did Pershing say of the American airplanes available to fight an air war?

Of the original 55 planes, Pershing had said: "Fifty-one were obsolete, and the other four were obsolescent!" Then the American industrial ingenuity took over. The American air force did a magnificent job during the closing months of the war.

412. Who was among the greatest aces in the American air force?

Eddie Rickenbacker, who became a Master Mason in 1922 in Kilwinning Lodge No. 297 of Michigan. He started as a chauffeur for Pershing (he had been an auto racer). By the end of the war he had been credited with shooting down 21 enemy planes, along with four balloons. He continued working for aviation, particularly with Eastern Airlines. During World War II he performed several special missions for America.

413. What future President of the United States was a battery captain during World War I?

Harry S. Truman. He took over a disorganized Battery D (from Missouri) and structured it into one of the best in France. Truman was a Missouri Freemason; most of the men in his battery were of Irish ancestry. These men would remain his loyal friends for life. (Also see more in a later chapter, and see *Brother Truman*.)

414. What did the book *200 Years* say about Truman and Battery D?

This Battery had "virtually destroyed the careers of three commanding officers." During a night fight, Truman's troops panicked. His horse stepped into a shellhole and threw Truman. When he got up he found his men fleeing. "I got up and called them everything I knew," he said. They returned to their positions, and Truman had no further problems with them. His officers said that no matter how filthy his men were, the fighting Past Master of Grandview Lodge No. 618 always looked neat and clean. One of his officers said that Truman always was clean shaven, "He must have shaved with coffee, because we didn't have plain hot water."

415. Did Freemasonry work with the Armed Forces during World War I?

It tried to, but was forestalled constantly. Although the Knights of Columbus, YMCA, and others were permitted to go overseas to work with the Armed Forces, the federal government refused to let Freemasonry do the same.

416. Why wouldn't the Federal Government permit Freemasonry to go overseas to provide social activities and moral support for **all** servicemen?

120   Masonic Trivia (and Facts)

The excuse most frequently given was that the government couldn't work with 49 or more Masonic entities. Raymond B. Fosdick, Chairman for the Committee on Training Camp Activities for the War Department, put it this way: "We absolutely cannot issue forty-nine separate permits to as many different Masonic Jurisdictions, to say nothing of the numerous other Masonic bodies. The best we could do would be to issue one permit to the Fraternity, under which all would have to come."

417. Who led the fight to try to have the government allow Freemasons to work overseas?

Townsend Scudder, a New York State Supreme Court Justice, and a Past Grand Master of Masons in New York. (For a complete account see *Freemasonry's Servant*, the story of The Masonic Service Association.)

418. Did President Woodrow Wilson get involved in the Masonic request to go overseas?

He did. And he agreed with Fosdick's opposition to the Masonic plan to aid the servicemen.

419. What eventually happened because of the government's refusal to permit Freemasonry to assist American servicemen?

George L. Schoonover, Grand Master of Masons in Iowa, became angry! On October 3, 1918 he sent a letter to every Grand Master in the United States asking them to meet with him in Cedar Rapids, Iowa. A short time later the meeting date was set for November 26-28, 1918.

420. Why was George Schoonover angry?

He had received a letter from a Masonic club in France wanting to know why American Freemasonry had ignored the servicemen. The letter pointed out how the Knights of Columbus, Red Cross, and other organizations had helped. Freemasonry, supposedly dedicated to helping all mankind, was nowhere to be found.

421. How many Grand Lodges were represented at the Cedar Rapids meeting? What did many of them learn for the first time?

Twenty-two were represented. Almost all of them learned for the first time that Freemasonry had been anxious to work with the Armed Forces overseas, but had been refused permission by the federal government. The reason? Because there was no unity within Freemasonry.

422. What was the great fear among the Grand Lodge representatives?

That unity would bring a General Grand Lodge into being. This was a dominant fear throughout the early days when they were discussing how they could best keep Freemasonry from being forbidden to help serve, in the name of all Grand Lodges, in times of calamity.

423. Was the fear of the formation of a General Grand Lodge eliminated?

After hours and days of discussion, the delegates voted unanimously to form a service organization for Freemasonry. A Constitution was finally drawn up to make certain this service association could never give birth to a General Grand Lodge.

424. How was the final resolution worded?

"*Resolved*, That there be organized the MASONIC SERVICE ASSOCIATION OF THE UNITED STATES, a voluntary association of Masonic Jurisdictions of the United States of America, for service to mankind."

425. How did the Grand Lodges react to the formation of The Masonic Service Association?

The acceptance of this service association was mixed. Even some of the Grand Lodges that were represented at the formation didn't officially agree to join. However, several that were not represented did join. And, amazingly, 34 of the 37 of these Grand Lodges were represented in 1919. Of the 12 other Grand Lodges, Virginia and Indiana had rejected the idea of the Association; the others had said nothing. Twenty-six of the attending delegations were headed by their Grand Master. It was the greatest sign of unity ever shown by the Grand Lodges of the United States.

426. What did the delegates to the meeting of the MSA adopt as its purposes?

The education of Freemasons, along with relief in times of distress, became the primary purposes.

427. When did the MSA start publishing *Short Talk Bulletins*?

The first *Short Talk Bulletin* appeared in 1923. It has been published monthly ever since then. Today one may be obtained an almost any Masonic subject.

428. What did the leadership of Freemasonry in the United States learn from the formation of the MSA?

It was found that Masonic jurisdictions could meet together without compromising their sovereignty. Consequently, in 1925 the first yearly Conference of Grand Masters was held in Chicago. This was followed also by a Conference of Grand Secretaries.

429. During its early years, what did the MSA accomplish?

It found excellent Masonic authors and writers, and published several fine Masonic books and digests. It proposed the development and publication of a Masonic encyclopedia. It found impressive motion picture producers, writers and actors to produce *Who Can Best Work* in 1923. It published an excellent magazine, edited by Joseph Fort Newton, called *The Master Mason*. (Microfiche of the entire series is now available from The Philalethes Society.) Film strips and Stereopitcon slides were made available to the Craft. It collected and distributed disaster relief funds for Japan, Florida and Mississippi.

430. Did the MSA continue to receive the support of the majority of the Grand Lodges?

It did not. In fact, it was almost destroyed. Forces worked to destroy the Association. What these forces were have never been determined. It is known that there was objection to the publication of books, but why this was so isn't understood. However, this opposition was so great, the rights to the books were sold to Macoy Publishing & Masonic Supply Co., Inc., in 1928.

431. What was the low point in the number of Grand Lodges remaining members of the MSA?

With only 14 Grand Lodges remaining members in 1928, Andrew Randall of Texas resigned as Executive Secretary. In 1929 Carl H. Claudy was elected as Randall's successor. In 1930 only eight Grand Lodges remained as members of the MSA.

432. Who was the Freemason selected to combat the increasing communist conspiracy?

J. Edgar Hoover, who became a Master Mason in Federal Lodge No. 1 in the District of Columbia on November 9, 1920. He entered service in the Department of Justice in 1917. In 1919 he became a special assistant to the attorney general to investigate and stifle any communist threat.

433. Who was a "power broker" in the Republican party during the Presidential nomination in 1920?

Harry M. Daugherty, a member of Fayette Lodge No. 107 of Ohio. He predicted the delegates would be deadlocked, and he would then present the name of Senator Warren G. Harding, a member of Marion Lodge No. 70 of Ohio. His prediction proved correct. Harding was nominated and later elected.

434. At the laying of a cornerstone in Birmingham, Alabama, what did President Harding say?

"I have been a better citizen for being a Mason. There is nothing in Masonry that a free religious and just American could not be proud to subscribe to, and be a better citizen for so doing."

435. Who was the Freemason accused in the "Teapot Dome" scandal?

Edwin Dewey, a member of Oriental Lodge No. 240 of Michigan. He was Secretary of the Navy. The scandal consisted, primarily, of leasing, without competitive bidding, oil reserves set aside in Teapot Dome in Wyoming in 1915 by President Wilson. Dewey wasn't found guilty. Others who were accused of bribery were convicted.

436. When and where did President Harding die?

Harding was scheduled to address several hundred Knights Templar in Hollywood, California, on August 2, 1923. He became deathly ill. His secretary, George B. Christian, a Knight Templar, read Harding's address. Three hours later, Harding died. Calvin Coolidge (not a Freemason), Vice President, was sworn in as President by his father in a farmhouse in Vermont.

437. Was the United State prosperous when Coolidge took over as President?

It was. Henry Ford, who was Raised in Palestine Lodge No. 357 of Michigan by a team composed of men wearing overalls, on November 28, 1894, had filled the roads, such as they were, with automobiles. John Fitch, who had been made a Freemason in Bristol Lodge No. 25 of Pennsylvania in 1785, had conceived the idea of steam, and this had brought prosperity through water traffic. Under the sea, submarines were trafficking, mainly because of another Freemason, Simon Lake of Monmouth Lodge No. 172 of New Jersey.

438. When was airmail service started?

A Postmaster General named Harry S. New, a member of Ancient Landmarks Lodge No. 319 of Indiana, established airmail service in 1918.

439. Who led the United States Marine Band for the decade of the 1880s?

For 12 years, from 1880 to 1892 the band was led by John Philip Sousa, who became a Master Mason in Hiram Lodge No. 10 in the District of Columbia on November 18, 1881.

440. Who were some of the Freemasons who came from "Tin Pan Alley?"

Irving Berlin became a Master Mason in Munn Lodge No. 190 of New York on June 3, 1910. Asa Yoelson, better known as Al Jolson, became a member of Cecile Lodge No. 568 of New York on July 1, 1913. George M. Cohan became a member of Pacific Lodge No. 233 of New York on November 16, 1905.

441. Was William F. Cody a Freemason?

Cody, known as "Buffalo Bill," became a Master Mason on January 10, 1917 in Platte Valley Lodge No. 32 of Nebraska. After a distinguished career as a federal scout during the Civil War, a pony express rider, Indian fighter in the battle of Wounded Knee, and owner of a wild west show, he was buried with Masonic Rites on Lookout Mountain, Colorado, on January 10, 1917.

442. Who was William Wyler?

Wyler was an academy award-winning motion picture director who directed, among many other films, the production of *Ben Hur*, written by a Civil War General Lewis Wallace, a member of Fountain Lodge No. 60 of Indiana. Wyler was a member of Loyalty Lodge No. 529 of California.

443. Who were some of the Freemasons enumerated by Henry C. Clausen in his booklet *Masons Who Helped Shape Our Nation*?

Clausen named as Freemasons: Douglas Fairbanks, Harold Lloyd, Frank Lloyd, Wallace Beery, Louis B. Mayer, Tom Mix, Hoot Gibson, James E. Blackmore, George Brent, Eddie Cantor, Joe E. Brown, Charles Coburn, Dan DeFore, Gene Autry, Will Rogers, Roy Disney, Cecil B. DeMille and Ernest Borgnine. For some reason, Clausen didn't mention Roy Rogers and a host of others involved in the motion picture industry.

444. Who opposed Calvin Coolidge in the Presidential election in 1924?

John W. Davis, a member of Herman Lodge No. 6 of West Virginia, was the Democratic candidate; Robert M. LaFollette of Madison Lodge No. 5 of Wisconsin was the candidate of the Progressive Party. Coolidge was elected.

445. What was the "Scopes Trial"?

A school teacher named John T. Scopes was accused of teaching the Darwinian theory of evolution! He was defended by Clarence

Darrow. The prosecutor was William Jennings Bryan, a member of Lincoln Lodge No. 19 of Nebraska. Bryan won a conviction, but it was overturned on a technicality. The trial took place in early July, 1925. Bryan died on July 26, 1925.

446. Who wrote *Letters of a Self-Made Diplomat to His President?*

William Penn Adair Rogers, better known as Will Rogers. He was a cowboy-humorist whose satiric wit entertained audiences for over a quarter of a century. He was also a columnist and an actor, appearing for several years in the *Ziegfeld Follies*. He received the degrees of Freemasonry in Lincoln Lodge No. 19 of Nebraska in 1902, and later affiliated with Temple Lodge No. 247 of Florida. He was killed in an airplane crash in Alaska, along with his friend Wiley Post, on August 25, 1935.

447. Who made the first non-stop solo flight across the Atlantic Ocean?

The largest headline in *The New York Times* on Sunday, May 22, 1927 read: "LINDBERGH DOES IT! TO PARIS IN 33 1/2 HOURS." It referred to Charles Augustus Lindbergh, Jr., who had flown his plane, "The Spirit of St. Louis" non-stop across the Atlantic. He wore a pin depicting the Masonic Square and Compasses. He was made a Master Mason in Keystone Lodge No. 243 in St. Louis, Missouri, on December 15, 1926.

448. Who was the naval officer who had flown over the North Pole?

Admiral Richard E. Byrd, a member of Kane Lodge No. 454 of New York. He, along with Floyd Bennett, had accomplished this feat in 1926.

449. Who received the Nobel Peace Prize in 1928?

Frank B. Kellogg, Secretary of State. He had been a member of Rochester Lodge No. 21 of New York since May 3, 1880. What became known as the "Kellogg-Briand Pact" (Briand was a Frenchman) was the "Pact of Paris" which outlawed war! This was signed by 62 nations in 1928, and included Germany, Italy, and Japan!!

450. What caused the "Great Depression" that began in 1929 and would bring a Freemason into the Presidency?

The New York Stock Exchange crashed on October 24, 1929, changing the lives of millions (including mine) forever. Alistair Cooke, the British author, wrote: "It became clear years too late that the torrent of liquidation [of stock] was caused, not so much by the big traders and bankers — who rushed in to try to plug the flood with twenty-five million dollars — but by legions of small-timers who had no margins to speak of."

451. Who won the Presidential election in 1932?

Franklin Delano Roosevelt, a member of Holland Lodge No. 8 of New York. He would later participate when his sons, Elliot, James, and Franklin were made Master Masons.

452. Who was the Republican candidate for the Presidency in 1936?

Alfred M. Landon of Kansas. He was a member of Fortitude Lodge No. 107. He received the electoral votes of only two states — Maine and Vermont.

453. What caused the demise of Freemasonry in Germany?

Nazism, under the control of Adolph Hitler who gained the mastery of Germany in 1933 and outlawed Freemasonry. It was learned years later that thousands of Freemasons, along with millions of Jews, were sent to German concentration camps and murdered.

13. War (Again) and Homes Away From Home

In these days of big money ... I might be excused if I were apologetic for the small sum [ten cents] asked of the two and a half millions of Freemasons of the nation. But, as a matter of fact, I am proud that the small contribution requested can go so far and do so much. I am proud because I know why it can do so much; proud that so many dedicated Masons are willing to give of their time and strength, sell their goods at cost, work for nothing or for a pittance, for the love of their fellow members of the oldest Fraternal organization in the world.

-Harry S. Truman-
In a nation-wide radio address, July 24, 1941

454. What was the top secret project that President Franklin Roosevelt authorized in 1940, thereby risking impeachment?

He authorized the development of an atom bomb. He also worked secretly with another Freemason, Winston Churchill of England, although the Congress had insisted on the United States remaining neutral. Roosevelt's efforts would be kept secret until the book *A Man Called Intrepid* (Sir William Stephenson) was written by William Stevenson, and published in the 1976.

455. What was happening to Freemasonry where Hitler's hordes reigned supreme?

Freemasonry was being suppressed and outlawed wherever the Nazis gained control. Like all despots, they believed that free men must be subjugated; dictatorships cannot survive where free thought and speech is permitted. Freemasonry, which believes in the freedom of man and the continuing search for truth, had to be destroyed.

456. Did Freemasonry in Germany capitulate?

Much of it did. A handful of dedicated Master Masons did keep the light of Freemasonry burning. An identifiable Masonic emblem could not be worn, so individuals in the Grand Lodge of the Sun in Bayreuth decided to have its members wear a little blue flower as a means of identification.

457. Has the wartime means of the German Masonic identification been perpetuated?

It has. In 1947 the Grand Lodge of the Sun adopted a lapel pin in the shape of a blue forget-me-not as its official emblem. In 1971 an organization was established to recognize those Freemasons who are writers and Masonic educators. It was felt these men are the backbone of the Craft, but far too often ignored. It was named "The Masonic Brotherhood of the Blue Forget-Me-Not." Its objective: to reward those of today who are keeping the light of Freemasonry burning. It also commemorates those dedicated German Masons who defied subjugation, even at the cost of their lives. Both groups have much in common.

458. While the Nazi juggernaut was overrunning countries in Europe, what was The Masonic Service Association doing?

Before he died in England in 1937, Jacob Hugo Tatsch, a Masonic author (among his books was *Freemasonry in the Thirteen Colonies)*, developed a plan for working with the Armed Forces in case of war. Under the leadership of Carl H. Claudy, Executive Secretary of The Masonic Service Association, the Executive Commission met and determined to ask the Grand Lodges to support Masonic aid for servicemen. The letter sent on November 1, 1939 read: "All, or a heavy majority of the Grand Lodges must cooperate, if they are not to be helpless, as in 1917-18. **The Masonic Service Association** is the voice Grand Lodges can command to speak their will."

459. What was the result of the appeal by the MSA for Masonic cooperation in the war effort?

Thirty-six Grand Masters endorsed the plan immediately; others felt their Grand Lodges should decide. The Grand Encampment, General Grand Chapter, Scottish Rite, NMJ, and Shrine also agreed to help and support the efforts of the MSA. These, plus other Grand Lodges, Grand Chapters of the Order of the Eastern Star, the Tall Cedars of Lebanon, the National League of Masonic Clubs, and the Order of Rainbow, would help the MSA assist the Armed Forces throughout the war. Not all Masonic-related bodies helped, but hundreds of individuals, along with some organizations not connected to Freemasonry, added their support. The war years were among Freemasonry's "finest hours."

460. Were all the Grand Lodges that helped in the MSA's war efforts members of the Association?

No. And many of them wouldn't join their sister Grand Lodges as members for a number of years. (One Grand Lodge, as of 1994, has never joined the MSA, and it didn't help during the war years.)

461. Where was the first of the MSA Masonic Service Centers opened?

Columbia, South Carolina, opened the first "Home Away From Home" on February 1, 1941. The Grand Lodge had contributed ten cents (or more) for each of its members to make the Service Center possible. It had the support of the War Department and the local citizens. It remained active throughout the war.

462. Did Freemasons in Hollywood help the war effort through the MSA?

They did. In April 1943 practically every studio in Hollywood contributed to the making of *Your Son is My Brother*. It was a first class production that told the story of MSA Field Agents working with and for servicemen in the "Homes Away From Home." Later the Hollywood film makers produced *To Aid and Assist*, a sequel to the first story. It portrayed what Freemasonry was doing to help servicemen who were patients in Veterans' hospitals. In 1975 Imagination Unlimited! produced *The Brotherhood of Man...*, an award-winner in international competition. It told the story of The Masonic Service Association.

463. Did the Freemasons in the Congress support the MSA's work for the Armed Forces?

They did. And Harry S. Truman, as Senator, Vice President, President, and finally as a private citizen supported the MSA until his death.

464. Did the MSA provide "Masonic cigarettes" for soldiers and sailors in hospitals?

Yes, thanks to the generosity of a cigarette manufacturer who was a Freemason. He provided specially packaged cigarettes to the MSA (and only the MSA) for this purpose. The Square and Compasses was not printed on the packages so no one could accuse anyone of exploiting the emblem.

465. Who was the French professor who before World War II gained the support of some Masonic leaders in the United States?

Bernard Fay wrote, among other books, *Revolution and Freemasonry* which was published by Little, Brown. He had the support of many within the Craft, and the story duped hundreds of its readers (and still does).

466. What did Bernard Fay do with the information about Freemasons that he had gathered?

The New York Times reported on December 5, 1946: "Bernard Fay ... was sentenced to life imprisonment at hard labor today on his conviction on a charge of intelligence with the enemy. M. Fay has been charged with publishing documents and lists of the Freemasons for the Vichy (Nazi dominated) government. This had resulted, according to the prosecution, in deportation or death for thousands of them." (The full story of Fay, insofar as it can be determined, is found in *Seekers of Truth*.)

467. What happened when the draft act was about to expire in August 1941?

General George C. Marshall, who had been made a Mason at Sight, and the President, among others, spoke of the dangers of letting the draft expire. It finally was extended. The vote, three months before the attack on Pearl Harbor, was 203 for, 202 against!

468. Were the Japanese living in the United States harassed or imprisoned?

Not really, except in California. The War Department urged the President to isolate Japanese in the United States. But it appears that only in California did this meet with support. The Attorney General of California, Earl Warren, a Past Grand Master of Masons, agreed, and many Japanese were sent to "relocation camps." Warren would, in 1953, become Chief Justice of the Supreme Court of the United States.

469. Was Freemasonry in France suppressed?

The Vichy (Nazi) government issued a decree on August 12, 1940 prohibiting all "secret societies." This was specifically aimed at Freemasonry. One of the cabinet members said all Masons should be "burned at the stake." All known Freemasons were arrested. Many of these were murdered or sent to concentration camps where hundreds died.

470. Was Freemasonry practiced in the concentration camps?

Amazingly, yes. In Buchenwald, for instance, a number of Freemasons met in secret, of course. At one point they even held a Masonic memorial service for one who had died. A few of them were appointed leaders. They worked up lessons, and one of them, classed as a nurse, would verbally carry these lessons from block to block.

471. Did Freemasons help others in concentration camps?

They did, but how much help they were able to give will never be known. In a Japanese prison camp in Java, Dutch Masons offered to act as sentinels when the Jesuits were meeting in secret. The offer was gladly accepted.

472. Who commanded the Chinese soldiers in Burma when the Japanese attacked and overran the country?

General Joseph W. "Vinegar Joe" Stillwell. He had been a member of West Point Lodge No. No. 877 of New York since June 1, 1916.

473. Who was commander of Armed Forces in the Philippines?

General Douglas MacArthur, who had been made a Mason At Sight on January 17, 1936.

474. Who was left to command the Armed Forces in the Philippines when MacArthur was ordered to go to Australia?

General Jonathan M. Wainwright was left with the unenviable task. He would become a Freemason in Union Lodge No. 7 of Kansas on May 16, 1946. The "battling bastards of Bataan" believed they were forgotten "and nobody gives a damn."

475. Was the Freemason from Missouri, Charles A Lindbergh's request to be reinstated in the air force accepted?

It wasn't. Roosevelt and others were still angered by Lindbergh's advice to stay out of the war. But Lindbergh, as a civilian, became a technical advisor to the Air Force, and he flew combat missions in the Pacific.

476. Who was one of the survivors of the Bataan Death March?

Harold K. Johnson, who would become a general and the Army Chief of Staff under President Lyndon Johnson (a Texas Entered Apprentice who never went further). General Johnson would become Director of Education and Americanism for the Scottish Rite, SJ.

477. Who was the early commander of the Army Air Force?

General Henry H. "Hap" Arnold, a member of Union Lodge No.7 of Kansas.

478. Who did General Arnold place in charge of the first bombing raid over Japan?

Colonel (later General) James Doolittle, who had become a Freemason in Hollenbeck Lodge No. 319 of California in 1918. The raid was made in specially refurbished B-25 medium bombers. They took off from the *U.S.S. Hornet,* which Roosevelt described as "Shangri-la," the mythical retreat of James Hilton's motion picture *Lost Horizon.*

479. Who was Chief of Naval Operations?

Admiral Ernest J. King, a member of George C. Whiting Lodge No. 22 of the District of Columbia since September 12, 1935. He fought for stronger operations in the South Pacific, but was overruled. The first priority was the war in Europe.

480. Who was the American flying officer fighting with the Chinese against the Japanese?

General Claire Chennault, who began fighting for the Chinese in 1937. In 1941 he formed a flying squadron of American volunteers called the "Flying Tigers." In the summer of 1942 this became the 14th Air Force. Chennault was a member of League City Lodge No. 1053 of Texas. He once noted his Masonic memberships ranged from Texas to China to California.

481. Who commanded the 5th Army in Italy?

General Mark Wayne Clark, who became a Master Mason in Mystic Tie Lodge No. 398 of Indiana.

482. Who was in command of the first amphibious landing on Tarawa in the South Pacific?

Colonel (later General) Merritt Edson, who became a member of Olive Branch Lodge No. 64 of Vermont on February 24, 1928. He gave his junior officers and their men full credit for their success in defeating the heavily entrenched enemy.

483. Who was the flag officer of Task Force 58 of the powerful Fifth Fleet in the battle of the Marshall Islands?

Admiral Marc A. Mitscher, who became a Freemason in Biscayne Lodge No. 124 of Florida on January 29, 1919.

484. Who was King of England during World War II?

King George VI, whose full name was Alfred Frederick Arthur George of the House of Windsor, gave his Brother Mason, Winston Churchill, who was made a Master Mason in Studholme Lodge No. 1591 in 1902, his full support throughout the war. The King was made a Mason in Naval Lodge No. 2012 in 1919. He was installed as Grand Master Mason of Scotland in 1936.

485. What happened to Freemasonry in Switzerland?

The Swiss Grand Lodge Alpina continued to work, and in the German language, during the Nazi terror. The Grand Lodge publication, which had been an internal organ since 1874, went public in 1938 to combat the anti-Masonic rhetoric. Remarkably, the Grand Lodge publicly and successfully celebrated its centennial on July 3 and 4, 1944.

486. What happened to Freemasonry in the Philippines?

In 1941 the Grand Lodge of the Philippines voted to help the allies. When the Japanese overran the Islands, they captured all known Freemasons and kept them imprisoned throughout the enemy occupation. How many were tortured and murdered will never be known.

487. Were all Fascists brutal?

It's important not to class any group as "all bad" or "all good." An example of tolerance appeared in a Fascist prison camp at Imperia, Italy. There a prison warden permitted Freemasons to meet, almost openly. Pierre Fraysee, a French Freemason and member of The Philalethes Society, said that many lectures on Masonic history were told to mixed groups. These "changed the opinion of Masonry of a good many non-Masonic prisoners."

488. When the United States troop ship *Dorchester* was torpedoed, what memorable action took place?

When the ship was abandoned, life jackets ran out. Four chaplains took off their jackets and gave them to servicemen. The chaplains went down with the ship. One of these men of God was George Fox, a member of Moose River Lodge No. 82 of Vermont. In

1951 a chapel in Philadelphia was dedicated to their memory. President Harry S. Truman addressed the audience. In 1993, fifty years after the sinking of the ship, a commemorative service was held in the Chapel.

489. What did French Freemasonry think of Franklin D. Roosevelt?

Evidently many admired the then President of the United States. A Lodge was formed in 1938 in Paris and named for FDR. The Grand Orient wouldn't permit a lodge to be named for a living person, so it changed. On June 15, 1945, after his death, it was again named in honor of the 32nd President. A memorial service was held on April 12, 1947. Over 1,400 were present to honor the memory of the Freemason who "saved civilization from servitude," and won the gratitude of all free men.

490. When was Mrs. Eleanor Roosevelt a guest of honor in Paris?

Franklin Delano Roosevelt Hall in Paris was dedicated on December 9, 1948. Mrs. Roosevelt was escorted into the hall by the Grand Master of the Grand Lodge of France, under "an arch of steel." When she rose to speak she received a long, standing ovation. She concluded by saying that she would never forget the enthusiastic reception of the French Freemasons. The Grand Master ordered a "triple battery to be given in her honor."

491. When did Harry S. Truman become the 33rd President of the United States?

Roosevelt died at Warm Springs, Georgia, on April 12, 1945. On the same day Truman took the oath of office as President.

492. Who started the Hospital Visitation Program in Veterans' Administration Hospitals?

In 1944 it became apparent that more than Masonic Service Centers were needed to help the Armed Forces. Carl H. Claudy, Executive Secretary, and John D. Cunningham, Chief Field Agent, of The Masonic Service Association proposed a plan for aiding hospitalized servicemen and women. The then Vice President, Harry Truman, agreed. So did members of the MSA Advisory Committee who were officers in the Armed Forces. The trial program became a permanent plan that exists today, with many other voluntary organizations participating.

493. When did the war in Europe end?

Surrender terms were signed by the German Admiral Karl Doenitz, who had succeeded Adolph Hitler who had committed suicide, on May 7, 1945. The war in Europe was over. But there was still heavy fighting in the Pacific.

494. Memorial Day 1945 would be one of the most meaningful in many years; when was "Memorial Day" first celebrated?

"Decoration Day," now known as "Memorial Day," was first observed on May 30, 1868. It was proclaimed by General John A. Logan, Commander of the Grand Army of the Republic (G.A.R.), and a member of Benton Lodge No. 64 of Michigan. A group from Chicago, while touring the battle torn countryside around Richmond, Virginia, noted the graves of Confederates were decorated with fading flowers. This was reported to Logan. He issued an order that all graves of fallen soldiers should be decorated on May 30, the date the last Union volunteer was discharged from service.

14. After the War

I commend the enviable record made during the war by the Association, acting as the agent for Grand Lodges and other Masonic bodies; especially am I interested in your plan for expansion of Masonry's Hospital Visitation service. Surely Freemasonry cannot do enough for those brave men who have sacrificed so much for our beloved country.
                              -President Harry S. Truman-
                                   Letter: January 6, 1946

495. What happened to the Masonic Service Center that had been opened in France?

The Paris, France, "Home Away From Home" that opened on April 8, 1945, proved to be just that. The Masonic Service Association planned on closing it in January, 1946, but the President of the Eiffel Tower Masonic club begged for it to remain open. Thousands of allied service men and women continued to pass through Paris. The Center was too popular to close, so it remained open for another year.

496. Was a Masonic Service Center opened in the Philippines?

In this one area, The MSA had to accept its only failure. Brother and General Douglas MacArthur told the Association: "I am in entire sympathy with the idea. Due to devastation here and other operational difficulties, the problem will not be an easy one to solve." After a year of work, surveying and correspondence, the plan had to be abandoned.

497. Did the work of The Masonic Service Association end with the end of war and the work of the occupation force?

No. The Veterans' Hospital Visitation Program it pioneered has been continued to the present day. And many other volunteer organizations joined in this endeavor. The MSA has continued its Masonic educational programs and its charitable work in times of distress.

498. What did many Freemasons in Hollywood do to help the MSA's Hospital Visitation Program?

To Aid and Assist, a motion picture previously mentioned, was produced which told the world about the need for the Visitation program. "It could not have been produced commercially! The men and women who made it ... did it for the love of doing it," said the Executive Commission.

499. How badly was Freemasonry in Europe harmed by the Nazi horror?

It was something President Truman and The Masonic Service Association wanted to learn. Through the President, a committee was selected to travel to Europe and submit a report to the President, the MSA, and the Masonic world. The committee left by air on April 12, 1945!

500. What was the result of the MSA committee's report on conditions in war-torn Europe?

The comprehensive report was sent to the President of the United States and every Grand Lodge in the country. Before the end of 1946, $123,535 had been sent to assist the Freemasons in ten European countries. CARE packages totaling 25,000 pounds were sent to European Grand Lodges for distribution to people in need. Over seventy thousand dollars was sent to the Philippines.

501. When did the world learn about how Freemasonry in Austria was affected by the Nazi regime?

The fact that Freemasonry as suppressed in Austria, and wherever the Nazi gained control, was known almost immediately. It wasn't until 1960 that a more detailed report was made public. Freemasonry had worked without obstruction until 1938. Then Hitler's forces took over the country and prohibited Masons from working.

Masonic temples were confiscated and Masonic leaders were thrown into prisons.

502. Why did the Freemason in the White House decide to use a virtually untested weapon against the Japanese?

Without question, this has been among the most controversial actions of World II. The derogatory objections have come mostly from those whose lives were not at stake. Throughout the Pacific the Japanese had strongly contested every section of ground they controlled. The battle for Okinawa had been especially bloody, a forerunner of what could be expected when Japan proper was invaded. It wasn't until Truman had assumed the Presidency that he learned of the "Manhattan Project" -- the making of an "atom bomb." After its successful test on July 16, 1945, at Alamogordo, New Mexico, the President knew he had an awesome decision to make. The loss of Allied lives in an invasion of Japan was estimated at one million; the Japanese would probably lose four or five times that many. On July 26, 1945 Truman issued a final ultimatum to the Japanese government. It was ignored. On August 6 the crew of the *Enola Gay*, a B-29 bomber, dropped an atom bomb on Hiroshima, Japan. The devastation and loss of life didn't cause the Japanese government to surrender. Another (the last) atom bomb was dropped on Nagasaki on the 8th. The Japanese government capitulated.

503. Who was the Freemason who was commissioned by another Freemason to accept the surrender of the Japanese?

Brother and General Douglas MacArthur was given the pleasant task by Brother and President Harry S. Truman. The terms of the surrender were accepted and signed aboard the *U.S.S. Missouri*, in Tokyo Bay, on September 2, 1945. The long struggle to regain freedom in the world was successfully ended.

504. Who first mentioned "an iron curtain"?

Brother Winston Churchill, in a speech in Fulton, Missouri, less than a year after the end of the war. The several countries behind that iron curtain were under the tight control of the Soviet government.

505. When and why was The Philalethes Society founded?

It was founded on October 1, 1928. Its founders were Masonic editors and writers who, in some cases, had their writings suppressed, "by those who held authority for a short time." They believed the truth concerning Freemasonry should be widely disseminated. The Society was formed "to create a bond of union for isolated Masonic writers and also to protect editors of Masonic publications.

506. When did The Philalethes Society publish the first edition of its magazine?

The first issue of *The Philalethes* was published in March, 1946.

507. What took so long for the Society to produce its own periodical?

For several years the Society had but little money. Its small number of members wrote articles in the name of the Society for other Masonic publications. During World War II its funds grew slightly, but paper wasn't available, and wouldn't be until 1946.

508. Has The Philalethes Society published its periodical continually since it started?

Except for a short period in 1952 *The Philalethes* has appeared bimonthly. Walter F. Quincke, one of the founders, became the President of the Society and Editor of the publication, but soon died. His successor also died shortly thereafter. For a period of several months the work of the Society became chaotic. Then Lee E. Wells, an historical novelist, and Alphonse Cerza, an Illinois lawyer, took over. John Black Vrooman began his long tenure as Editor. The publication of the magazine has continued on schedule ever since.

509. Did the Grand Lodges in the United States welcome the Grand Lodges of Europe after the war?

Let Melvin Maynard Johnson, Past Grand Master of Masons in Massachusetts and Grand Commander of the Scottish Rite, Northern Masonic Jurisdiction, answer this question. Writing for *The Philalethes* in the July 1948 issue, he took exception to "some ultra-conservative Masonic leaders concerning the recognition of European Grand Lodges." It appeared that some Grand Lodges questioned the legitimacy of some of these Grand Lodges. He wrote: "Personally, I would rather be associated with a bastard who is himself a moral, upright good man than with one of legitimate birth who is a crook and a scoundrel."

Regarding stability: "It seems to me to be self-evident that the time to help with treatment and nursing is while one is sick and needs help, instead of waiting until he is either cured or dead."

Legality: "Few sovereign States, even of the English-speaking world, have expressly declared the legality of Freemasonry. No American is a real Freemason, no matter what jewels he many wear, if he idly watches the destruction of Freemasonry and its ideals in other lands when he, with his brethren, has the opportunity of being a good Samaritan."

Conclusion: "It is regrettable but true that there are those of official station in all large organizations whose action in important as well as trivial matters is governed by selfishness rather than that pure altruism which Freemasonry teaches. From those we are not exempt."

510. Who was Melvin Maynard Johnson?

Johnson served as Grand Master of Masons in Massachusetts in 1914-16. He became Grand Commander of the Scottish Rite, Northern Masonic Jurisdiction, and under his leadership his jurisdiction established a foundation for research into the causes of schizophrenia, which began in 1934 and continues strongly active today. He received the highest Masonic awards of many Grand Lodges. He was a staunch supporter and friend of Harry S. Truman. He established the Gourgas medal as the NMJ's highest award. Johnson wrote several articles and books, including *The Beginnings of Freemasonry in America.*

511. Who was the first recipient of the highest award of the Scottish Rite, Northern Masonic Jurisdiction?

Senator Harry S. Truman was elected in 1943 to be the first to receive this highest award of this body. It was in recognition of his work for Freemasonry and his devotion to duty as a United States Senator in the war effort. Because of Truman's busy schedule the presentation couldn't take place until November 21, 1945, after he had become President of the United States. The medal honored the memory of John J. J. Gourgas (1777-1865), the first Secretary General and the third Sovereign Grand Commander of the NMJ.

512. Who became Administrator of Veterans Affairs for the Veterans Administration after World War II?

Brother and General Omar N. Bradley, who became a member of West Point Lodge No. 877 of New York in 1923. He told the Congress that he would accept the position, but only if he could work "for the benefit of service men and not for the purpose of providing political pork for anyone." Bradley had fought throughout World Wars I and II. He was Army Chief of Staff in 1948 and 1949; Chairman of the Joint Chiefs of Staff from 1949-53.

513. What was the "Truman Doctrine"?

To help combat the destitution in Europe, Truman determined to support "free people who are resisting attempted subjugation by armed minorities and by outside pressure." Based on this premise, the European construction program came into being. Many would call this "The Marshall Plan" (George C. Marshall was Truman's Secretary of State). Truman hoped the resulting contribution of over twelve billion dollars to this effort would prevent another senseless world war.

514. Who opposed Truman in the Presidential election of 1948?

Three other Freemasons! The Republican candidate was Thomas E. Dewey, a member of Kane Lodge No. 454 of New York. On the Progressive ticket was Henry A. Wallace, a member of Capital Lodge No. 110 of Iowa since 1927. The States Right Democratic ticket was headed by J. Strom Thurmond of Concordia Lodge No. 50 of South Carolina. To the astonishment of almost everyone but Truman, President Truman won!

515. Who was the United States general whose funeral service was conducted by a Japanese Lodge?

General Walton H. Walker was a member of Belton Lodge No. 166 of Texas when he was killed in Korea on December 23, 1950. He had earlier told his troops: "There will be no more retreating, withdrawal, or anything else you want to call it," and there wasn't. At the request of the Walker's wife, Star of the East Lodge No. 640 of Yokahama, Japan, conducted the Masonic funeral service for him.

516. Why did President Truman fire his commander in Korea?

Brother and General Douglas MacArthur didn't appreciate the orders he had received from the President, so he wrote a letter to the minority leader of the House of Representatives. The letter was released to the press. The President said he could no longer tolerate MacArthur's insubordination. He relieved MacArthur of his command on April 11, 1951.

517. What happened to MacArthur when he returned to the United States?

MacArthur received a hero's welcome. Speaking before a joint session of the Congress, he concluded: "Old soldiers never die, they just fade away." Truman reached a new low in the opinion polls.

518. What was found when the President had the White House restored?

Brother and General Henry H. Vaughan, the President's military aide, found a stone in the rubble with Masonic markings on it. He reported this to Truman. A search was made. More than 100 other marked stones were discovered. These had been built into the original "President's Home" whose cornerstone had been laid with Masonic ceremonies on October 13, 1792. During 1953, the President had one of these stones delivered to each Grand Lodge and other selected places.

519. When was the Grand Lodge of Israel constituted?

On October 20, 1953, by the Grand Lodge of Scotland. Frenchmen had brought Freemasonry to the area in 1902 during the building of the Suez Canal.

520. Who was the first American to orbit the earth in a space craft?

John H. Glenn, Jr., on February 20, 1962. In 1964 Glenn petitioned and was elected to receive the Masonic degrees in Concord Lodge No. 688 of Ohio. But, for varying reasons, it would be August 19, 1978, before he would become a Master Mason. On that day the Grand Lodge of Ohio officers conferred each of the three degrees on him. He then became a full fledged member of Concord Lodge.

521. Who created and published *The Royal Arch Mason* magazine?

Ray V. Denslow, who served as presiding officer of virtually all Grand Bodies in Missouri. After his death on September 11, 1960 his son, William R., continued its publication.

522. During the formation of the United States, who were the governors who were Freemasons?

This was a continuing question, and often exaggerated. James R. Case again answered it in December 1960 in the pages of *The Philalethes*. As of July 4, 1776 there were three: Archibald Bullock of Georgia; Richard Caswell of North Carolina; and Henry Laurens of South Carolina. As of October 19, 1781 there were two: Nathan Brownson of Georgia; and John Hancock of Massachusetts. On April 20, 1789 there were five: George Walton of Georgia; John Hancock; John Sullivan of New Hampshire; Alexander Martin of North Carolina; and Thomas Chittenden of Vermont. There is no proof that Thomas Nelson of Virginia and John Eager Howard of Maryland were Freemasons.

523. What caused Gregory Ratoff, the film actor and director to became a Freemason?

Darryl Zanuck told Ratoff how he and others carried the body of John Adolphi, packed in ice, home from a hunting trip. Adolphi had suffered a fatal heart attack. They carried his body to his home so his widow wouldn't have to wait to collect his insurance. The coroner demanded positive prove of Adolphi's identity. He found it in the pocket of the jacket on the body—a Masonic membership card with Adolphi's picture. At the railroad station at the small Canadian town of Revelstoke 100 Freemasons in Masonic regalia met Zanuck's party as they departed for California. Ratoff determined then he wanted to be a Mason. And Ratoff was buried with Masonic rites in February 1960.

524. When was it announced that Henry Wilson Coil had finally completed his *Masonic Encyclopedia*?

During the Workshop of The Philalethes Society on February 24, 1961 it was announced that Coil, a Fellow of the Society, had completed his long task, and the encyclopedia would be published by

Macoy Publishing & Masonic Supply Co. It would be 1994 before a revised edition of Coil's remarkable work would be published.

525. Who was among the first to publicly state that Prince Hall Masonry is legitimate?

George E. Bushnell of the Northern Masonic Jurisdiction of the Scottish Rite said Prince Hall Masonry is legitimate. This was in answer to a series of question during a court case in Philadelphia in 1961. In answer to a further question, Bushnell said his jurisdiction considered no "other Negro Masonic body in the United States" as being legitimate.

526. What was one of President Lyndon B. Johnson's orders after being sworn in as President of the United States?

President John F. Kennedy was assassinated in Dallas, Texas, on November 22, 1963. Johnson (who had received only the Entered Apprentice degree) took the oath of office aboard *Airforce* One. He ordered the Federal Bureau of Investigation to check every aspect of the assassination. The FBI had long been headed by J. Edgar Hoover, a member of Federal Lodge No. 1 of the District of Columbia.

527. Who was selected to head the special commission to investigate Kennedy's assassination?

The Chief Justice of the Supreme Court of the United States, Earl Warren, was chosen to head the commission. Warren was a Past Grand Master of Masons in California. Two other Freemasons were on the commission: Senator Richard B. Russell, a member of Winder Lodge No. 33 of Georgia; and Gerald R. Ford, a member of Malta Lodge No. 465 of Michigan.

528. Who was the Republican candidate who opposed President Johnson in the Presidential election of 1964?

Barry Goldwater, a member of Arizona Lodge No. 2, was the Republican candidate who was "destroyed politically" by Bill D. Moyers and Doyle Dane. According to Patrick Anderson in his *The President's Men*, they, at the instigation of Johnson "directed the most vicious media attack in political history." It was Dane who produced the "Daisy Girl" TV picture of a small blond child picking petals from a daisy when suddenly a giant mushroom-shaped nuclear cloud engulfed the child. This was but one of the continuing attacks against Goldwater that cost him the election.

529. Who were some of the early "space travelers" who were Freemasons?

Walter M. Schirra, Jr., L. Gordon Cooper, Jr., Thomas P. Stafford, Edwin E. Aldrin, Jr. (in 1969 he would become the first human to step foot on the moon), and Virgil I. Grissom. Grissom was killed in a capsule accident on January 27, 1967.

530. Who were the Vice Presidents of the United States who were Freemasons?

In April 1970 *The Philalethes* listed the Masons who had served as Vice President as: General George Clinton, Eldridge Gerry, Daniel K. Tompkins, Richard M. Johnson, George Millflin Dallas, William Rufus King, James C. Breckenridge, Andrew Johnson, Schuyler Colfax, Adlai E. Stevenson, Garrett A Hubart, Theodore Roosevelt, Charles W. Fairbanks, Thomas R. Marshall, Henry A. Wallace, Harry S. Truman, Hubert H. Humphrey, and Gerald R. Ford. Three of these, Tompkins, Dallas and Truman, had served as Grand Masters.

531. Who was one of the most prolific authors of Masonic and other works who died in 1964?

Roscoe Pound, a Past Master of Lancaster Lodge No. 54 of Nebraska. He became a Freemason in 1901, and it is claimed he learned the catechism of the first degree on his way home from the Lodge! He would later be elected an Honorary Past Grand Master. After his death on July 1, 1964 it was found that the bibliography of his writings filled more than 245 pages! Many of his Masonic works are still consulted.

532. What has finally been determined to be the oldest Masonic hall still in existence in the United States?

Masons Hall in Richmond, Virginia, was determined to be the oldest Masonic building. The long going debate about the claim of Royal White Hart Lodge of North Carolina was settled in the pages of *The Philalethes* in 1968. The cornerstone of Masons Hall was laid in

1785 and the building is still in use, exclusively, by Richmond Randolph Lodge No. 19, and Richmond Chapter No.3, Royal Arch Masons. It was the first permanent home of the Grand Lodge of Virginia. It was 1821 before Royal White Hart Lodge moved into its own building.

15. Onward

Freemasonry's simplicity, its dignity, and its spirituality sustain me in all that I try to do, and permit me to forget the incredible pettiness of mind that we sometimes encounter, *sustaining me and enabling me to join hands with my brethren everywhere, to do something, if it be only a little, before the end of the day, to make a kinder and wiser world in which to live.*

-Joseph Fort Newton-

533. The *U.S.S. Pueblo* was captured by North Korea on January 23, 1966. Who were two of the Senators who condemned the Johnson administration's inaction?

After the unarmed ship was captured, President Johnson's lack of action was condemned by many. Among them was Everett M. Dirksen, a member of Pekin Lodge No. 29 of Illinois, and J. Strom Thurmond of Concordia No. 50 of South Carolina. It would be eleven months before the crew was freed from captivity by the North Korean government.

534. Who was the Presidential candidate who was seriously wounded in 1972 in an assassination attempt?

George C. Wallace, Governor of Alabama, was campaigning for the Democratic nomination for President when he was shot on May 15, 1972. He was left paralyzed from the waist down. He had served as Orator of the Grand Lodge of Alabama in 1961.

535. At the Workshop of The Philalethes Society in February 1972 it was announced that Conrad Hahn would receive the James Royal Case Medal of Excellence. Who was Conrad Hahn?

Conrad Hahn was a Past Grand Master of Masons in Connecticut. He became the Executive Secretary of The Masonic Service Association of the United States in 1964, after serving as its Deputy Executive Secretary for two years. He became one of the most loved and knowledgeable Freemasons in the country. Under his leadership the MSA grew in the number of member Grand Lodges. He died suddenly in December 1977.

536. Who was James Royal Case?

James Case was one of the foremost Masonic historians of his day. He specialized in researching the Masonic membership of the Revolutionary period. For years he was the historian of all the Masonic bodies in Connecticut. To honor him the Medal of Excellence of the Connecticut Masonic Research Lodge bore his name.

537. Who were the recipients of the Medal of Excellence?

All recipients were Fellows of The Philalethes Society: James R. Case, Conrad Hahn, Harold V.B. Voorhis, Dwight L. Smith, Ronald E. Heaton, Alphonse Cerza and Allen E. Roberts.

538. Who was the prominent Catholic clergyman who believed Catholic Freemasosns should not be excommunicated?

Dr. John A. O'Brien, of the University of Notre Dame. In an article he wrote for *The Philalethes* in June 1972 he said for Freemasons who believed in God and obeyed the landmarks of the Craft there would be no reason for excommunication. He quoted Jesuit Father Jean Beyer of the University of Rome who said Masons shouldn't be excommunicated if they "should reveal themselves as believers in God and defenders of their government."

539. When did Harry S. Truman die?

Truman died on December 26, 1972 in his home in Independence, Missouri. He was 88 years young.

540. Did President Truman have a Masonic funeral?

The government assumed the details of Harry Truman's funeral. He did not have the Masonic funeral he had requested, but a five minute Masonic service was permitted. Grand Master W. Hugh McLaughlin presented a beautiful Masonic testimonial to a nationwide television audience. (For complete details on Harry S. Truman as a Freemason, Politician and statesman, see *Brother Truman*.)

541. Where was President Truman buried?

Truman is buried at the Harry S. Truman Library in Independence, Missouri.

542. Where did the money come from to build the Truman Library?

Not a cent came from the government. Truman gave every dollar he received for speaking engagements to the foundation established to build the Library. And, incidentally, he was the last President to receive no government funds, secret service agents, or money for office space or staff, nor pension. When the library was completed, Truman and the foundation turned it over to the government.

543. Who was chosen to head the "Watergate" committee?

Senator Samuel J. Ervin, Jr., a member of Catawba Lodge No. 17 of North Carolina, was chosen to head the investigation that would finally cause President Richard M. Nixon (not a Freemason) to resign his office. This began as a minor break in to "bug" Democratic headquarters in the Watergate building on June 17, 1972. The media helped turn the charge into a Presidential "cover up."

544. How many Freemasons participated in the Vietnam "police action"?

No one knows how many Freemasons were involved in Vietnam. It began when President Lyndon Johnson sent "advisors" to aid the South Vietnamese. It ended (somewhat) when the first former prisoners-of-war arrived at Clark Air Force Base in the Philippines on February 13, 1973. Among them were: Captain Melvin Pollack, a member of Hope Lodge No. 244 of New York; Major Paul J. Montague of Anthony No. 200 of Kansas; Lieutenant Colonel Dewey W. Waddall of Bremen No. 456 of Georgia; Colonel James E. Bean of Duvall No. 6 of Kentucky; and Major Jerry Singleton shortly after his return became a Master Mason in A.C. Garrett Lodge of Texas.

545. When was ground broken for the library and museum of the Scottish Rite, Northern Masonic Jurisdiction, in Lexington, Massachusetts?

On February 5, 1973 ground was broken for what would become the Library and "Museum of our National Heritage." It was officially opened on April 20, 1975. It was noted that it was a gift to the American people and admission would be free at all times.

546. After Spiro T. Agnew resigned as Vice President, who was chosen to replace him?

Gerald H. Ford, a member of Malta Lodge No. 465 of Michigan, was sworn in as Vice President of the United States on December 6, 1973.

547. When did Brother Gerald Ford assume the Presidency of the United States?

Richard Nixon's resignation took effect at noon on August 9, 1974. Shortly before noon, Ford took the oath of office from Chief Justice Warren Burger (not a Mason).

548. Of the statues of great men in the District of Columbia, how many are of Freemasons?

In his lecture when he was made a member of the Society of Blue Friars in 1973, Ralph A. Gauker enumerated the "Statues of Great Masons in Our Nation's Capital." Thirty-nine "have definitely been established as being of Master Masons." Seven are of Past Grand Masters: Thomas Hart Benton of Iowa; Lewis Cass of Ohio and Michigan; Henry Clay of Kentucky; Benjamin Franklin of Pennsylvania; Andrew Jackson of Tennessee; William King of Maine; and George L. Shoup of Idaho. He didn't name the others, but did mention George Washington at length.

549. Why was Harry S. Truman memorialized by the Order of DeMolay during April 1973?

For many years Brother Truman had been the Honorary Grand Master of the Order of DeMolay. His work as the leading Freemason of the country was also commemorated.

550. During 1973 what was learned about why Hitler condemned Freemasonry?

According to Hermann Rauschnigg, in his *Gesprache Mit Hitler* (Conversations With Hitler), Hitler knew Freemasonry was harmless, but because his party "must be something similar, an order, an hierarchic organization of secular priesthood," such as Freemasonry, could not continue to exist. He said the Catholic Church opposed Freemasonry. "Now we are the strongest and, therefore, we shall eliminate both the Church and the Freemasons."

551. What did the Islamic World Congress do in 1973?

This congress asked the Islamic world to ban "British originated speculative Freemasonry." It succeeded. However, during the Persian Gulf war (1990-91), when dozens of countries, including most Islamic ones, banded to fight the aggression of Iran, many members of the American-Canadian Grand Lodge located in Saudi Arabia provided aid to the Freemasons stationed in that country.

552. Who was Henry Wilson Coil?

Coil was a California Freemason and lawyer who devoted much of his adult life to writing for Freemasonry. He died on January 29, 1974 at the age of 89. His funeral was conducted by Riverside Lodge No. 635. His painstaking Masonic research will live forever, especially his mammoth Masonic encyclopedia that was published in 1961. During his lifetime he never received the credit he deserved.

553. When was the last Presidential plaque (at least, until 1994) placed in the George Washington Masonic National Memorial?

On February 17, 1975 a plaque depicting the portrait of Gerald R. Ford was placed among those of the other Presidents who were Freemasons. At the time he said: "Let us today rededicate ourselves to new efforts as Masons and Americans. Let us demonstrate our confidence in our beloved Nation, and a future that will flow from the glory of the past."

554. Who are Presidents who were Freemasons whose plaques are in the George Washington Masonic National Memorial?

George Washington, James Monroe, Andrew Jackson, James Knox Polk, James Buchanan, Andrew Johnson, James Abram Garfield, William McKinley, Theodore Roosevelt, William Howard Taft, Warren Gamaliel Harding, Franklin Delano Roosevelt, Harry S. Truman and Gerald Rudolph Ford.

555. What is the George Washington Masonic National Memorial?

The idea for a lasting monument to the first President of the United States was conceived in 1910 by Alexandria-Washington Lodge No. 22 of Virginia. It was supported by, and is the property of, all the Grand Lodges (and consequently all of the Freemasons) of the United States. It is located on Shooters Hill in Alexandria, Virginia. It is the symbol of the universality of Freemasonry.

556. Where can the best account of Freemasonry during the Revolutionary period be found?

From 1974 to 1983 Freemasonry during the Revolutionary period was covered at length in the pages of *The Philalethes* magazine of The Philalethes Society. Excerpts from these accounts will be found in *Seekers of Truth*, the sixty year history of the Society. Much that occurred in Masonic circles during the 200th anniversary celebration in the United States will also be found within those pages.

557. Who was the Republican candidate for Vice President in 1976?

Robert Dole, a member of Russell Lodge No. 177 of Kansas, was selected by Ford to be his running mate. They lost the election to James Earl "Jimmy" Carter (not a Mason).

558. After the Congress, at the insistence of President Carter, voted to turn the rights to the Panama Canal over to Panama, how was Freemasonry affected?

The "treaty," as written, would have given Panama all of the property in that country. This would include that of Sojourners Lodge, the only privately owned property in Panama. The Lodge, after many failures, reached Senator and Brother Dole's office. An aide of Dole's, Robert L. Downen, a member of Albert Pike Lodge No. 177 of Kansas, took the documentation of the Lodge to Dole. This was presented to the State Department, which again turned down the Lodge's request to keep its property. Dole's threat to Carter and the State Department to include an amendment to exclude the Lodge property from the "give-away" worked. The final version of the treaty gave the Lodge its rightful land. The Lodge later elected Dole and Downen to Honorary Membership.

559. What happened to Freemasonry in Iran when the Shah was forced to leave his country?

Shah Mohammed Reza Pahlevi, a Freemason and friend to Freemasons, was forced to leave Iran on January 16, 1979. With his departure, Freemasonry, which he had supported, was squelched. He had made a fatal mistake in allowing the Ayatollah Ruhollah Khomeini to return to the country. Khomeini took over the dictatorship of Iran and abolished all freedom. On November 4, 1979, with the approval (and perhaps instigation) of Khomeini, the American embassy compound was broken into and the Americans taken hostage. They would remain hostages until Ronald Wilson Reagan (not a Mason) was sworn in as President of the United States on January 20, 1981.

560. When was the Grand Lodge of Alaska formed?

It was formed by twelve Lodges holding charters from the Grand Lodge of Washington on February 5, 1981 when its Constitution was adopted. Its officers were installed on the 6th; it held its first communication on the 7th.

561. When did a Grand Lodge return to Spain?

Dictator Franco had persecuted known Freemasons after he gained control of Spain in 1936. In the 1960s Freemasonry was practiced on American military bases. With the death of the dictator, Spanish Freemasons became somewhat active. Finally, on November 6, 1982 a Grand Lodge was instituted by officers from the Grand Lodge National.

562. What is the only Masonic memento in the *USS Arizona* Memorial at Pearl Harbor, Hawaii?

After months of negotiating, the General Grand Council, Cryptic Masons, International, presented a plaque to the Memorial on July 9, 1983. It reads: "In memory of the more than 2400 brave Americans who lost their lives during the attack on Pearl Harbor December 7, 1941. ALOHA."

563. What did the Grand Lodge of California do for visitors to the Olympic Games in 1984?

The Grand Lodge opened and manned a "Masonic Host and Information Center" in Los Angeles. Among its many conveniences was a short wave radio unit to allow guests to send messages to their homes around the world.

564. When was the Grand Lodge of Hawaii formed?

With the blessings of the Grand Lodge of California, from whom the Lodges in Hawaii had received their charters, the Grand Lodge of Hawaii was instituted on May 20, 1989. It was the last state within the United States to form its own Grand Lodge. Every state, plus the District of Columbia, is now a Masonic jurisdiction unto itself.

16. Toward the Next Century

It really is a piece of unmitigated humbug on the part of the Church of England to issue a report criticising Freemasonry. In the days when the Church could boast men of stature among its bishops, even archbishops found it not incompatible with their Christian convictions to belong to the Masonic Order....

Having been a member of the Church of England all my life and a Freemason for twenty-four years, I feel a great sadness that the Church is no longer able to set out its tenets as clearly, concisely and unambiguously as does Freemasonry.
Rev. Eric E. Gaunt, June 26, 1987
Church Times, England

565. What happened to Prince Hall Masonry in Liberia in 1980?

Rebel forces that took over the country, on April 12, 1980, mutilated and murdered a Past Grand Master. Other Prince Hall Masons were stripped, lashed, and then shot. Masonic halls were destroyed or seriously damaged. It would take eight years before Prince Hall Masonry could become active in the country once again.

566. What caused the Church of England, and other such organizations, to condemn Freemasonry?

The principal cause was a book written by Stephen Knight called *The Brotherhood*. The book, published in 1984, was loaded with so many falsehoods about the Craft, it's amazing to believe that any intelligent person could take them seriously. But the book prompted the publication of many comments on Freemasonry, both friendly and hostile. Most of the favorable comments about Freemasonry that went to the religious publications were written by clergymen, many of these ministers were not connected to the Fraternity.

567. How did the publication of Knight's book, and the subsequent attacks by religious fanatics, affect the United Grand Lodge of England?

The Grand Lodge began a public relations program. Freemasons' Hall in London was more fully opened to the public. The work of the Freemasons throughout the country was frankly discussed. Prior to this period, this Grand Lodge, and others, frequently ignored all criticism of the Craft. The theory appeared to be, such protests, if dismissed, would go away.

568. What historic action took place among Freemasons in Washington state on September 12, 1987?

Over 2,000 Masons from the Grand Lodge of Washington and the Prince Hall Grand Lodge of Washington marched together to celebrate the 200th anniversary of the adoption of the Constitution of the United States. The Grand Master said: "What a sight! Two thousand Masons marching together, six abreast, in a seemingly endless line.... It was a sight and a thrill I shall never forget." Three years later, each Grand Lodge would officially recognize the other.

569. Is the Reverend Jesse Jackson a Master Mason?

On May 21, 1987 the Grand Master of the Illinois Prince Hall Grand Lodge officiated during a meeting where Jesse Jackson became a Freemason in that Grand Lodge.

570. Who was the judge whose appointment to the Court of Appeals was held up because he was a Freemason?

Judge David Bryan Sentelle was nominated on April 8, 1987 for the Court of Appeals. Because he was a member of Excelsior Lodge No. 60, Senators Patrick Leahy and "Ted" Kennedy, and others, objected to his confirmation. On September 9, 1987 he was confirmed by a vote of 87 to 0, with 13 not voting! Many of the Senators who are Freemasons strongly supported Sentelle's decision to not renounce his Masonic membership. As the judge would later say: "If I were to give up my membership ... it would be like saying I had done something wrong in all the years I had been a judge; I would have been repudiating the principles that led my father, my grandfather, my uncles and my brother into this Fraternity." In 1988, Virginia's Grand Master Donald M. Robey, MPS, permitted Cherrydale Lodge No. 42 to elect Sentelle to Honorary Membership in the Lodge.

571. What did The Philalethes Society do to celebrate its 60th anniversary?

On October 1, 1988 a gala banquet was held in Richmond, Virginia, with members and their ladies from all over the country in attendance. New awards were approved and presented to worthy Freemasons. *Seekers of Truth*, its 60 year history, was distributed to every member of the Society. Chapters throughout the United States and Canada held special affairs.

572. What did Dr. Norman Vincent Peale say in Iowa on February 21, 1988 about the criticism of Freemasonry ?

"That doesn't bother me at all because the criticisms aren't founded on reality. The critics know nothing about which they speak. I would like to make a prophecy that Freemasonry will be here 1,000 years from now, and Freemasonry is composed of the finest God fearing, moral men I have ever known in my life." He concluded: "... so, if people attack Masonry, always remember *nobody kicks a dead horse*. It's a sign of life, vitality, strength. Just keep on being Freemasons as we've always known it and the problem will take care of itself." Dr. Peale, a world renowned Christian Minister, was a Fellow of The Philalethes Society. He died on December 24, 1993.

573. Was President Ronald W. Reagan made an "honorary Freemason"?

During his last days in office in 1987, Reagan was presented with a certificate of honor from the Grand Lodge of the District of Columbia -- this did not make him a Mason by any stretch of the imagination. The Scottish Rite Bodies and the Shrine gave him honorary membership in these bodies. From the point of view of Masonic jurisprudence, this was improper. One must be a Master Mason to be considered for membership in any appendant body.

574. What did the "Islamic Resistance Movement-Palestine" say it was going to do to Freemasonry?

According to *The Washington Times* of November 16, 1988, this Islamic group said, "When Islam gains control of its destiny, it will liquidate these organizations [Freemasonry, Rotary, Lions and other 'Zionist-affiliated' organizations], which are anathema to humanity and Islam." Freemasonry had been abolished in all Islamic countries before this "movement" gained control!

575. Was William Shakespeare really the author of the works that bear his name, and did he write some of the Masonic ritual?

This controversy about who wrote his works was settled (or was it?) in 1988, when three British judges ruled that Shakespeare, and not Edward de Vere, or any other writer, did the job. But this controversy won't go away. For years it has been known that Shakespeare wrote no Masonic ritual. Those who did write portions of the early ritual were familiar with the works of the English bard and freely used some of his terminology.

576. When did the postal service recognize William F. Cody?

William F. Cody, better known as "Buffalo Bill," was honored by the postal service with the issuance of a stamp bearing his likeness on June 6, 1988. Cody became a member of Platte Valley Lodge No. 32 of Nebraska on January 10, 1871.

577. What did a bungling Congress do to "Buffalo Bill"?

It took away the Congressional Medal of Honor he had earned! Here's part of the story: William Cody had served as an Indian scout during the American Civil War, and again in 1868 to 1872. It was in this latter year that he led a cavalry charge against a band of Sioux Indians. For his bravery beyond the call of duty he was awarded this highest award. But he was a civilian! Congress, in its usual wisdom, decreed in 1917 that only military men were eligible for this award, and it was made retroactive! Cody was stripped of his award. Then, in July 1989, the medal was rightly restored to Cody, who had died on January 10, 1917.

578. On what Bible did George Herbert Walker Bush take the oath as President of the United States?

On January 29, 1989 Bush (not a Mason) took the Presidential oath of office on the same Bible Brother George Washington had used 200 years earlier. The Bible is owned by St. John's Lodge No. 1 of New York City. This same Bible was used by Brother Warren G. Harding, Dwight D. Eisenhower (not a Mason), and James Earl Carter (not a Mason, and using the name of "Jimmy").

579. When was the Grand Lodge of Hawaii instituted?

On May 20, 1989 the Grand Master was elected and the Grand Lodge officers "unofficially installed." The official installation took place on July 1, 1989. For years the Freemasons of Hawaii were under the jurisdiction of the Grand Lodge of California. It welcomed its daughter into the fold of world-wide Grand Lodges.

580. The December 1989 cover of *The Philalethes* magazine featured the "Poinsettia." What's the Masonic story behind this flower?

The flower is named for Joel R. Poinsett, a Past Master of Recovery Lodge No. 31 of South Carolina, and Solomon's No. 1 of South Carolina. As the first United States Ambassador to Mexico he found this flower and brought it to the U.S. It is said there are between 700 and 1,000 species of the Euphorbia pulcherrima, and it has many uses, including dye and medicine.

581. Which American Grand Lodge first recognized Prince Hall Masonry as a legitimate Masonic body?

On October 14, 1989 the Grand Lodge of Connecticut and the Prince Hall Grand Lodge of Connecticut voted to recognize each other as legitimate Masonic bodies and to permit intervisitation. Both would remain an independent Grand Lodge. The Grand Lodge of Nebraska did the same on February 3, 1990. On June 20, 1990 the Grand Lodge of Washington and its Prince Hall counterpart mutually agreed to intervisitations. So have those of Wisconsin, Colorado, North Dakota, Minnesota and Idaho.

582. When was the Grand Lodge of Hungary reactivated?

Communist authorities abolished Freemasonry in Hungary in

1950, and confiscated all Masonic regalia and property. On August 15, 1989 a Grand Master was elected. Officers of the Grand Lodge of Austria installed the Grand Lodge officers of Hungary on December 27, 1989.

583. Which "special" Lodge in Indiana Raised its 100th candidate in 1990?

Bartimaeus Lodge, U.D., established in 1962 to work with handicapped candidates, Raised its 100th man on April 14, 1990. Its officers are trained to handle special infirmities.

584. The well-known business analysis, Standard and Poor's ran a survey in 1990. What did it find?

According to *The Indianapolis Star* of July 23, 1990, the survey found that executives are getting younger. And "The composite picture of the typical U.S. business executive is that of a 48-year-old man who works in New York, is president of a company and belongs to a Masonic order."

585. What historical Masonic event took place in Walla Walla, Washington?

On June 8, 1991 a headstone with Masonic emblems was placed on a grave. What made this unusual? It was placed at the head of the grave of William Upton who had urged the Grand Lodge of Washington, while he was Grand Master, to recognize Prince Hall Masonry. Before he died he said no headstone was to be placed at his grave until his Brothers, of whatever color, could march side by side. On this day, as over 400 black and white Freemasons walked side by side to Upton's grave, he might have smiled and said: "How good and how pleasant it is for Brethren to dwell together in unity."

586. Who was the famous American Freemason who was killed in an automobile accident in 1991?

Jerald Edmond "Jerry" Marsengill was killed in a still unexplained auto accident on November 22, 1991. He was returning from having been inducted into St. Joseph Conclave, Red Cross of Constantine, in Missouri. For years Marsengill was the spark plug that made Iowa Research Lodge No. 2 one of the best in the country.

He edited *The Philalethes* from 1976 and was its editor at the time of his death. He was also the editor for *The Royal Arch Mason* magazine. He was a Past President of The Philalethes Society, a member of the Society of Blue Friars (Masonic authors), an original member of The Masonic Brotherhood of the Blue Forget-Me-Not (Masonic educators), a Past Grand Master of the Grand Council of Cryptic Masons of Iowa, a Past Grand High Priest, a Past Grand Chancellor of the Grand College of Rites. He was in demand as a speaker throughout the country.

587. Who was the famous English Freemason who was the Lecturer for The Philalethes Society in 1992?

Cyril N. Batham was the Philalethes Lecturer on February 14, 1992. Among his other Masonic honors, Batham was the Prestonian Lecturer in 1981. He is a Past Master of Quatuor Coronati Lodge No. 2076 and was its Secretary for a number of years. From 1975 to 1985 he edited the Transactions of this Lodge. The Queen admitted him to the Order of St. John. He holds Grand Rank in England, France and Spain. He has lectured in many countries.

588. When was a charter awarded for the first Computer Chapter of The Philalethes Society?

In 1992 a Masonic forum was opened on a world-wide computer service called "CompuServe." Since then Freemasons from all over the world have joined in Masonic discussions. Shortly after the formation of the Forum, the Executive Board of The Philalethes Society authorized the formation of "Cornerstone Computer Chapter." The charter was presented during the Annual Assembly/Feast/Forum of the Society on February 18, 1993. Freemasons from all over the world join in discussions about Freemasonry.

589. What statue of a famous Freemason did a faction in the District of Columbia attempt to have removed?

In 1898 authorization was approved to place a statue of Albert Pike on public land in the District. In 1992 a faction headed by a prison inmate named Lyndon LaRouche, attempted to have it removed, claiming Pike was (among other unsavory things) a member of the Ku Klux Klan (although there is no proof of this). Many of the leaders in Prince Hall Masonry supported the efforts to keep the statue, and its still stands. Pike was prominent in Scottish Rite circles, and much of what he wrote and envisioned about the degrees for the Southern Jurisdiction is followed today.

590. Who wrote the newspaper article, "Calling Masons Satanic is Folly," and why?

The article was written by a non-Mason named Paul Harasim for *The Houston Post* of February 24, 1993. He was writing about a dentist named James Holly who had led the Southern Baptist Convention into considering a resolution condemning Freemasonry as a work of the devil. The writer pointed out how ludicrous Holly's charges were. This action did have one good object—it brought together the Masonic leadership as nothing else ever has. During the convention, the resolution didn't reach the floor. However, a report by a committee to study Freemasonry was approved, which in essence agreed that membership in Masonry is left to the conscience of the individual. Actually, this is the way it has always been.

591. What outstanding event took place at Gettysburg, Pennsylvania, in 1993?

For the first time a private organization was permitted to erect a monument in a national park. The monument, a gift of the Grand Lodge of Pennsylvania, depicted a Freemason, Federal Captain Henry Bingham, aiding his mortally wounded Brother, Confederate General Lewis A. Armistead. Engraved on the base is "Friend to Friend—A Brotherhood Undivided." It is estimated that over 35,000 were present on August 21, 1993 when the monument was dedicated by officials of the Grand Lodge.

592. In which Monastery does a Research Lodge meet?

With the blessing of Abbot-Bishop George Burke, a Freemason and member of The Philalethes Society, St. John the Baptist Research Lodge meets in the Holy Protection Orthodox Monastery in Geneva, Nebraska. On July 3, 1993 the Lodge hosted the Grand Masters of the Grand Lodge of Nebraska and the Grand Master of the Prince Hall Grand Lodge.

593. Who was the outstanding comedian honored by the Grand Lodge of Indiana?

On November 20, 1993 Richard B. "Red" Skelton received the Grand Lodge of Indiana Award of Gold. Skelton had been Raised in Vincennes Lodge No. 1 on September 20, 1939. The celebration lasted for more than two hours; Skelton, in his inimitable style, "regaled his guests with never ending bursts of jokes and anecdotes and tales of his boyhood in Vincennes."

594. Is Freemasonry a "secret society?"

This was a question asked of the thousands of Freemasons using the Masonic Forum on CompuServe. Many of their responses were published in *The Northern Light* of the Northern Masonic Jurisdiction in August 1994. The overwhelming consensus is "Freemasonry is not a secret society" in the strictest sense of the term. However, in those countries that abhor freedom, Freemasons must, indeed, be discreet. One respondent said: The terms "secret society" and "society with secrets" should be expunged from the Masonic vocabulary.

17. Potpourri

An hour with a book would have brought to his mind
The secret that took him a whole year to find.
The facts that he learned at enormous expense
Were all on a library shelf to commence.
Alas! for our hero, too busy to read,
He was also too busy, it proved, to succeed.
We may win without energy, skill, or a smile,
We may win without credit, or backing, or style,
Without patience or aptitude, purpose or wit --
We may even succeed if we are lacking in grit;
But take it from me, as a mighty safe hint,
A civilized man cannot win without print.
-Anonymous-
in Seekers of Truth

595. What's **The Funniest Language You Ever Did See?**

We'll begin with a box, and the plural is boxes
But the plural of ox is oxen, not oxes.
Yet the plural of mouse should never be meese!
Then one fowl is a goose, but two are called geese!
You may find a lone mouse or a whole nest of mice,
Yet the plural of house is houses, not hice!
If the plural of man is always men,
 Why shouldn't the plural of pan be called pen?
If I speak of a foot, and you show me your feet,
And I give you a boot -- would a pair be called beet?
If one is a tooth, and a whole set are teeth,
Why should not the plural of booth be called beeth?
Then one may be that and three would be those,
Yet hat in the plural would never be hose,
 And the plural of cat is cats, and not cose!
 We speak of a brother, and also of brethren,

But though we say mother, we never say methren!
Then the masculine pronouns are he, his and him,
But imagine the feminine, she, shis and shim!
So, English I fancy, you all will agree,
Is the funniest language you ever did see!
-Anonymous-
The Philalethes, February 1973

596. What is often considered the best limerick of all time?

Dixon Lanier, made a Mason in Owensboro Lodge No. 130, Kentucky, later affiliating with Corinthian No. 414 in Tennessee, wrote in 1913 what would become a widely circulated limerick. It reads:

A wonderful bird is the pelican!
His bill will hold more than his belican.
    He can take in his beak
    Food enough for a week,
But I'm damned if I see how the helican.

597. What horrifies editors more than any other one thing?

The typographical error is a slippery thing and sly.
You can hunt till you are dizzy, but it somehow will get by.
Till the forms are off the presses, it is strange how still it
    keeps;
It shrinks down into a corner and it never stirs or peeps.

The typographical error, too small for human eyes,
Till the ink is on the paper, when it grows to mountain size.
The boss he stares with horror, then he grabs his hair and
    groans;
The copy reader drops his head upon his hands and moans—
The remainder of the issue may be clean as clean can be,
But the typographical error is the only thing you see.

598. Where can the original "Lodge of the Holy Saints John" (referred to by Senior Wardens in some rituals) be found?

Nowhere! Rumors have run rampant for many years about this "lodge" and its location. Most prevalent was that it was located over Clerkenwall Gate in London, England. Harry Carr of England was asked to investigate this claim. He found it "pure imagination run riot." The archway, with the room it encloses, still spans the road, and it was used as a Lodge room from about 1750 to 1880, but has had no Masonic connection for almost 100 years.

599. Who was the printer of what is perhaps the world's most famous Bible?

he printer was the inventor of movable type which made it possible for books and articles to be easily copied. His name— Johannes Gensfleisch zur Laden—better known by his mother's name —Gutenberg!

600. Who was the Masonic author who conducted his own funeral?

Harold Van Buren Voorhis died on May 23, 1983. He had been the founder and supporter of many of the "little Masonic bodies" meeting annually in the District of Columbia. For over 50 years he had been a ham radio operator and had used tape recorders since they were first invented. By way of a tape recorder, he conducted his own funeral! And not only in the church, but at his grave side! He said he was taking away this burden from his survivors, and he had conducted his own prayers and made his peace with God.

601. What is the structure of a Masonic Lodge?

According to an Anonymous source the officers' structure follows:
>MASTER:
* Leaps tall buildings in a single bound
* Is more powerful than a locomotive
* Is faster than a speeding bullet
* Walks on water
* Gives policy to God
>SENIOR WARDEN:
* Leaps short buildings in a single bound
* Is more powerful than a switch engine
* Is just as fast as a speeding bullet
* Walks on water -- if the sea is calm
* Talks with God
>JUNIOR WARDEN
* Leaps short buildings with a running start

* Is almost as powerful as a switch engine
* Is faster than a speeding BB
* Walks on water on an indoor swimming pool
* Talks with God -- if his special request is approved

SECRETARY
* Lifts buildings and walks under them
* Kicks locomotives off the tracks
* Catches speeding bullets in his teeth, then eats them
* Freezes water with a single glance
* He is a step higher than God

602. Is Freemasonry a difficult organization to join?

It can be! This story gives one version: A man was checking in at a Hotel, and while at the Registration desk, he noticed a group of men heading toward a function room.
He said to the Clerk, "Who are those men?".
She replied,"Oh, they're the Masons. They are meeting in one of our function rooms until their new Lodge is finished."
He replied, "Oh yeah, the Masons! Isn't that the group that's so hard to get into?"
She replied, "You don't know the half of it!. See that man with the sword? He's been banging on that door for eight months and they haven't let him in yet!"

603. Can Freemasonry compete for attendance with television and other entertainment activities?

It can, but only in one way. A Masonic Lodge has only one thing to offer its members that they can't find anywhere else. This is Freemasonry! Which means the Lodge must provide MASONIC programs for its members and visitors. These can include good, informative, entertaining Masonic speakers; good Masonic plays; debates; discussions; question and answer forums; and on and on.

604. Who were the four distinguished men receiving the 33° of the Scottish Rite on the same day?

On October 19, 1945 Harry S. Truman, General Douglas MacArthur, General Henry H. "Hap" Arnold and General James H. "Jimmy" Doolittle received the 33° of the Scottish Rite.

605. What was "The Masonic Editor's Vow" that was printed in *The Cabletow* of the Grand Lodge of the Philippines in 1927, and reprinted by the Editor of *The Philalethes* in 1959?

> I am firmly resolved: To write only that which is clean and true and for the best interest of the Craft; to endeavor to instruct and enlighten the readers of my paper; to let Brotherly Love, tolerance and charity guide me in my judgment of persons, things and events; to be temperate in expression, show fortitude under attack, display prudence in dealing with questions of moment, and endeavor to do justice to all, whether friend or foe.
> I will not mock or belittle that which others firmly believe to be right, just and holy, nor will I hurt the feelings of any person, great or small, if I can help it.
> I will not allow my judgment and policy to be influenced by mercenary motives, but will proceed without fear or favor and prefer honest poverty to ill-gained affluence.
> Towards my colleagues of the press I will ever be courteous and honest, abstaining from borrowing their thoughts and ideas and copying their work without giving due credit in each case, and I will do all I can to bring Masonic journalism to the high level which it should and must occupy.

606. Were the vigilantes in early Montana Freemasons?

All evidence points to most, if not all, of these protectors of the innocent being members of the Craft. After gold was discovered at Grasshopper Creek (later named Bannock) all types of unsavory characters appeared. Among them was a lawless sheriff. A group of Freemasons requested a dispensation from the Grand Lodge of Kansas to form Virginia City Lodge. Shortly after this request, some of these men met and took the following oath:

> We, the undersigned uniting ourselves in a party for the laudible purpos of arresting thieves & murders & recover stollen property, do pledge ourselves upon our sacred honor each to all others do solemnly swear that we will reveal no

secrets, violate no laws of right & never desert
each other or our standard of justice so help us
God, as witness our hand & seal this 23 of
December A.D. 1863.

These men finally caught the sheriff and four of his associates in a lawless act. They were hanged. The code "3-7-77" (still used by the Montana State Patrol) became a death warrant for the criminal recipient. It is said the numerals mean that the lawless may occupy graves *three feet wide, seven feet long, and seventy-seven inches deep.* The vigilantes made it possible for the law abiding to go about their business in peace.

607. When did the Grand Lodge of the Philippines recognize the Grand Lodge of Japan?

On July 8, 1958. This paved the way for recognition by other Grand Lodges throughout the world.

608. Who perpetrated the greatest hoax ever on the Roman Catholic Church and Freemasonry?

Throughout history there have been thousands (actually, millions) of "hoaxers." They exist in great numbers today, raking in billions of dollars from the unwary. Many of these are stealing hundreds of thousands of dollars peddling their lies about Freemasonry. Perhaps the greatest of these was Gabriel Antoine Jogand, a Frenchman and prolific writer using the pen name Leo Taxil. He was born in Marseilles on March 23, 1853. On August 1, 1881, after Taxil had written several books, he was ordered to stand trial for unMasonic conduct. Among the books cited was *The Secret Love Affairs of Pope Pius IX* (English translation), which Taxil didn't consider a Masonic offense, but the trial commission did, terming it the selling "of obscene material." At the end of the trial, Taxil was permanently expelled from Masonry. The "anti-cleric" and pornographer also became the "anti-Mason." Combining all of these together wouldn't prove difficult for this man with a vivid imagination. Earlier he had an instrument made for one of his lectures. He claimed it was a "spider" which the Inquisition used to tear out women's breasts. This proved to be one of his milder anti-clerical hoaxes.

After his expulsion from Freemasonry (he was an Entered Apprentice) he told the clerics he had recanted and was accepted by the

Church when he said he would write anti-Masonic books. Among his greatest hoaxes was the creation of "Miss Diana Vaughan of South Carolina." He claimed she was born in 1874, and was the daughter of the devil. She became a member of a masonic lodge, and later married the devil. Month after month "she" (in the person of Taxil) issued copies of documents reciting events of the satanic masonic lodges, of which she was a member. "Diana" received thousands of letters praising her revelations about the evils of masonry.

In Trent, in September 1896, Cardinal Parocci held an "Anti-Masonic Congress" to which a large number of the Catholic hierarchy was invited. Those few who saw through Taxil's hoax were denounced as heretics. Then, at the Geographical Society in Paris on Easter Monday, 1897, Taxil told a large crowd that Diana Vaughan had never existed! He had to be protected from an outraged mob. The Church remained unusually silent, but Abel Clarin de la Rive, wrote in the 1897 issue of *Freemasonry Dissected:*

> With frightening cynicism the miserable person we shall not name here declared before an assembly especially convened for him that for twelve years he had prepared and carried out to the end the most extraordinary and most sacrilegious of hoaxes. We have always been careful to publish special articles concerning Palladism and Diana Vaughan. We are now giving in this issue a complete list of these articles, which can now be considered as not having existed.

609. To get a job done, who do you give it to?

> If you want to get a favor done
>   By some obliging friend,
> And want a promise, safe and sure,
>   On which you may depend,
> Don't go to him who always has
>   Much leisure to plan;
> But if you want your favor done,
>   Just ask the busy man.
>
> The man with leisure never has
>   A moment he can spare,
> He's always "putting off" until
>   His friends are in despair.
> But he whose every waking hour
>   Is crowded full of work,

Forgets the art of wasting time.
    He cannot stop to shirk.

So when you want a favor done
    And want it right away,
Go to the man who constantly
    Works twenty hours a day.
He'll find a moment sure, somewhere,
    That has no other use,
And fix you while the idle man
    Is framing an excuse.
            -Anonymous-

610. When was a Masonic meeting held on the Antarctic Continent?

Seven officers and petty officers, including Lieutenant Commander F.G. Dustin, who recorded the event, met "at the bottom of the world" on February 6, 1947. They met in a flimsy canvas hut amidst a raging blizzard.

611. What is one of the interesting Arab Proverbs?

He that knows not, and knows not
  that he knows not is a fool. Shun him.
He that knows not, and knows that he knows
  not, is an honest man. Help him.
He that knows, and knows not that he knows,
  is asleep. Wake him.
He that knows, and knows that he knows, is
  a wise man. Follow him.

612. What did Freemasonry have to do with the Royal Canadian Mounted Police?

"The Mounted Police" act was passed in 1873 by the Canadian Parliament. That Fall 150 men marched across uncharted prairies to MacLeod, Alberta. This was named for the first Commissioner of the force, a Freemason. In 1905, "Royal" was added to the name. In 1920 it became "The Royal Canadian Mounted Police." In Regina in October 1894 Northwest Mounted Police Lodge No. 11 was instituted. In the early years only members of the force were permitted to join the Lodge.

Later the membership became so scattered, "outsiders" were permitted to join. The motto of the force became *"Maintiens le Droit."*

613. Was John Paul Jones a Freemason?

John Paul (who would later add his uncle's name "Jones") was made a Freemason in St. Bernard's Lodge No. 122, Kirkcudbright, Scotland, on November 27, 1770. Houdon made a bust of Jones for the Lodge of Nine Sisters in Paris, France. He died in Paris on July 18, 1792, and was buried in the Protestant Cemetery there. For over 100 years his body remained in this resting place, then it was conveyed to America. In 1913 it was placed beneath the domed Naval Chapel at the U.S. Naval Academy at Annapolis, Maryland. It is said that no other Naval Commander had so elaborate a tomb. Among the cherished mementos is John Paul's letter requesting admittance to the Scottish Lodge (there were no formal petitions then).

614. Did Theodore Roosevelt really sit in his Lodge with Elihu Root?

Elihu Root wasn't a Freemason, so the story about Theodore Roosevelt sitting in his Lodge with his Secretary of State is false.

615. Did Freemasons assist destitute children in South Korea?

The Pusan Masonic Club of South Korea was composed mainly of United States Servicemen. In 1951, during the "police action" in that country, members of this club laid the framework for a children's hospital. Monetary support was continued from Freemasons in the United States.

616. What was the prayer prayed by a stalwart pro-Masonic minister?

"Oh, Lord, bless this glorious Order; bless its friends; yea, bless its enemies, and make their hearts as soft as their heads. Amen."

617. Was the cornerstone of the extension of the East Front of the United States Capitol laid with Masonic rites?

The Grand Lodge of the District of Columbia laid this cornerstone on July 4, 1959. President Dwight David Eisenhower (not a Mason) said: "So long as we never waver in our devotion to the values on which these men began the building of the Nation, no differences of partisan policy or partisan feelings can cause America to falter on her upward course."

618. What has Freemasonry done for the youth in colleges and universities?

In 1897 a Square and Compass club was formed at Washington and Lee University at Lexington, Virginia. It received a charter from the state on May 17, 1917 under the name "Square and Compass Fraternity." Fifty-seven Collegiate Squares (chapters) were established. In these, about 5,000 men were initiated. These included men who were Grand Lodge officers, college and university presidents, public officials and businessmen. In 1950 the name as changed to "Square and Compass—Sigma Alpha Chi." Sigma Mu Sigma was formed by Freemasons at Tri-State College, Angola, Indiana, in 1921. These two fraternities were united on August 3, 1952. "The Collegiate Order of the Golden Key" was first conferred at the University of Oklahoma on March 21, 1925. The ritual, written by a college Mason, was conferred on Grand Lodge officers and Past Grand Masters.

619. Why does Freemasonry teach by symbols?

For the same reason this answer can be interpreted in many ways. Freemasonry leaves every member free to determine his own conclusion as to the meaning of any symbol. Man has used symbols for teaching for thousands of years. Symbols are still found, not only in Freemasonry but in every religion and industry. (You have just put together many symbols and put them together into words that have been decoded by your brains.)

620. When and where did Admiral David G. Farragut die?

The Admiral died on Sunday, August 14, 1870 at the navy yard in Portsmouth, New Hampshire. His funeral was held on the 17th. St. John's John Lodge, with many members of St. Andrew's Lodge and many others, were in attendance. Among them were U.S. troops, heavy artillery and marines. Religious services were conducted in St. John's church, followed by a Masonic service at a tomb in the church yard. At the conclusion of the service, fifteen volleys were fired.

621. Now that Freemasonry is slowly entering the field of computer record keeping, of what must it be aware?

Computer operators must take into account the dangers of the usually excellent means of checking the spelling of documents. Witness this jingle titled "Spellbound" written by Pennye Harper:
I have a spelling checker;
It came with my PC;
It plainly marks for my revue
Mistakes I cannot sea.
I've run this poem threw it,
I'm sure your pleased too no.
It's letter perfect in it's weigh;
My checker toiled me sew.

622. What is the "Baal's Bridge Square"?

During the excavation of Baal's Bridge over the river Shannon in Ireland, a square was found within the foundation. It read: "Upon the Level, by the Square / I will strive to live, With love and care. 1507." This relic is in the possession of Lodge of Limerick No. 13 in Ireland. To add to its probable Masonic authenticity, it was found under the eastern corner of the northern land pier (the northeast corner!).

623. What were the "Schaw Statutes"?

In 1593 Schaw was appointed Master of Work and General Warden of Masons by King James VI. The first set of his statutes were circulated to all Scottish lodges in 1598. These two codes of rules established the government of Scottish Masons.

624. What is a Trestle Board?

According to most rituals in the United States, the "Trestle Board" is what the operative Master of masons drew his designs upon. The Speculative Master uses this "board" to outline his plans for his Lodge. Many English and other Masonic rituals call this object a "Tracing Board."

625. What does "So Mote It Be" mean?

This is the oldest phrase still used by Freemasons, and is found in the *Regius Poem* of about 1390. It is usually used to close a prayer, and means "So may it be" or "Amen." It may also be used to close a serious Masonic work, such as this, by writing

So Mote It Be

About the Author

Allen E. Roberts was among the first to earn the title of "Certified Administrative Manager." In 1969 he started Imagination Unlimited!, a motion picture company that specialized in working with fraternal organizations, especially Freemasonry. In 1981 he added a subsidiary, Anchor Communications, that specialized in publishing books about and for Freemasonry.

He was born in Pawtucket, Rhode Island, on October 11, 1917. There he attended public schools. He was among the first to enter the Civilian Conservation Corps, where he became a Medical Assistant. He worked as a baker, and then a pastry chef in a large hospital in Providence, Rhode Island. After the bombing of Pearl Harbor he enlisted in the U.S. Navy where he earned five medals and five battle stars. He was a Chief Commissary Steward when he was discharged at the end of World War II. Governor George Wallace later appointed him a Lieutenant Colonel Aide- de-Camp on his staff in the Alabama State Militia.

He has made his home in Highland Springs, Virginia, "on the sacred ground where part of the Seven Days Battle during the Civil War was fought." He continued his studies in journalism, accounting, business law and banking at various institutions, including T.C. Williams Law School. He is listed in several of Marquis' *Who's Who* and *Who Is Who In Freemasonry*.

He has been recognized by several Grand Lodges with medals and citations. In 1994 the Grand Lodge of Virginia dedicated "The Allen E. Roberts Library and Museum" in recognition of his work for the Craft. Among the citations presented at this time was one from The Masonic Service Association commending him for his years of work for it.

Bibliography

Allen, Hervey, *City in the Dawn*, Rinehart, NY, 1950

—*Bedford Village*, Rinehart, NY, 1950

American Military History, Department of the Army, U.S. Government Printing Office, DC, 1956

Borneman, Henry S., *Early Freemasonry in Pennsylvania*, Grand Lodge of Pennsylvania, 1931

Carr, Harry, *Freemason At Work*, The, Revised by Smyth, Frederick, 7th edition, Lewis Masonic, 1992.

Carter, James D., *Masonry in Texas*, Grand Lodge of Texas, 2nd ed., 1955

Centennial Celebration, Grand Lodge AF&AM of Colorado, 1961

Child, Dr. William, *A History of the Fifth Regiment New Hampshire Volunteers, in the American Civil War*, Bristol, NH, 1893

Clausen, Henry C., *Masons Who Helped Shape Our Nation*, AASR, SJ, 1976

Coil, Henry Wilson, *Freemasonry Through Six Centuries*, 2 vols., Missouri Lodge of Research, MO., 1966-68.

—*Coil's Masonic Encyclopedia*, Macoy, VA, 1961

Cooke, Alistair, *America*, Alfred A. Knopf, NY, 1973

Denslow, William R., *10,000 Famous Freemasons*, Missouri Lodge of Research, 1960-62

Ford, Gerald R., *A Time to Heal*, Harper & Rowe, NY, 1979

Fort, Joseph Fort, *River of Years*, (an Autobiography), Lippincott, 1946.

Gottschalk, Louis, *Lafayette in America*, U. of Chicago, 1975

Gould, Robert Freke, *History of Freemasonry*, 3 vols., John C. Yorston, NY, 1885.
(This is by far the most authentic history of the Craft yet published. All subsequent accounts have not contradicted his findings and most have not expanded on them.)

Grand Lodge of Scotland Year Book, Grand Secretary, Edinburgh, various issues.

Grand Lodge, 1717 - 1967, various authors, United Grand Lodge of England, Oxford, 1967.

Graybill, Ben W. (edited by Forrest D. Haggard), *History of Kansas Masonry*, Grand Lodge of Kansas, 1974

Guthrie, Charles Snow, *Kentucky Freemasonry, 1788-1978*, Grand Lodge of Kentucky, 1981

Haywood, Harry L., *Wellsprings of American Freemasonry*, MSA, 1973

Heaton, Ronald E., *Masonic Membership of the Founding Fathers*, MSA, 1965
—and Case, James R., *The Lodge at Fredericksburg*, Heaton, PA,1975

Johnson, Melvin M., *Freemasonry in America Prior to 1750*, MA 1916

—*The Beginnings of Freemasonry in America*, Doran, NY, 1924

Lang, Ossian, *History of Freemasonry in New York*, Grand Lodge of New York, 1922

Langston, LaMoine, *A History of Masonry in New Mexico*, 1977

Leaves From Georgia Masonry, various authors, third printing, Grand Lodge of Georgia, 1970

Lennhoff, Eugen, *The Freemasons*, (originally published in German as *Die Freimaurer*, 1930), A. Lewis, Shepperton, England, 1978.

Little Masonic Library, various authors (originally edited by Carl H. Claudy), 5 vols., Macoy, VA, 1977

McLeod, Wallace, *The Grand Design*, Anchor Communications, VA, 1985.

Mellor, Alec, *Stange Masonic Stories* (From the French *Histoire des Scandales Maçomniques*), Macoy, VA, 1985

Newton, Joseph Fort, D.D. *River of Years*, J.P. Lippincott, NY, 1946

Parramore, Thomas C., *Launching the Craft*, Grand Lodge of North Carolina, 1975

Philalethes, The, Various Issues, 1946-1984

Pick, Fred L., Knight, G. Norman and Smyth, Frederick, *Freemason's Pocket Reference Book, The*, Third (revised) Edition, Frederick Muller, London, 1983.

—*Pocket History of Freemasonry, The*, Fifth edition, Frederick Muller, 1969.

Pollard, Ralph J., *Freemasonry in Maine*, Grand Lodge of Maine, 1945.

Prichard, Samuel, *Masonry Dissected*, England, 1730, facsimile published by the Masonic Book Club, IL

Reguis Manuscript, The, a facsimile published by the Masonic Book Club, IL, 1970 (originally written [or copied] c. 1390).

Roberts, Allen E., *Freemasonry in American History*, Macoy, VA, 1985

—*Freemasonry's Servant*, The Masonic Service Association, 1969

—*Frontier Cornerstone*, Grand Lodge of Ohio, 1980

—*G. Washington: Master Mason*, Macoy, VA, 1976

—*House Undivided*, Macoy, VA 1961 / 1990

—*Key to Freemasonry's Growth*, Macoy, VA, 1969.

—*The Saga of the Holy Royal Arch of Freemasonry*, motion picture, General Grand Chapter of Royal Arch Masonry, Int'l, 1974

—*Seekers of Truth*, Anchor Communications, VA 1988

Robinson, John J., *Born in Blood: The Lost Secrets of Frreemasonry*, Evans, NY, 1989.

Scotland, Grand Lodge Year Book, Grand Secretary, Edinburgh, various issues.

Rugg, Henry W., D.D., *History of Freemasonry in Rhode Island*, Grand Lodge of Rhode Island, 1895.

Singer, Herbert R., *New York Freemasonry*, Grand Lodge of New York, 1981.

Smith, Dwight L., *Goodly Heritage,* Grand Lodge of Indiana,1 968

Smith, James Fairburn, *Dateline 1764: Michigan Masonry*, Grand Lodge of Michigan, 1979.

Tatsch, J. Hugo, *Freemasonry in the Thirteen Colonies*, Macoy, 1929

200 years, two volumes, U. S. News and World Report, DC, 1973

Voorhis, Harold V. B., *Facts for Freemasons,* Macoy, VA, 1979

Walkes, Jr., Joseph A., *Black Square andCompass*, Macoy, VA, 1979

Wesley, Charels H., *Prince Hall, Life and Legacy,* United Supreme Council, SJ, PHA, and Afro-American Historical and Cultural Museum, PA, 1977

Whence Come We?, McLeod, Wallace E., Editor, Grand Lodge A.F. & A. M. of Canada in the province of Ontario, 1980.

Wilkinson, John C., *History of the Grand Lodge of A. F. & A. M. of Oregon*, Grand Lodge of Oregon, 1952 (with additional chapters through 1977)

Index

Aberdeen Lodge, Scotland, 5, 8, 29
Abraham Lodge, Kentucky, 65
A.C. Garrett Lodge, Texas, 153
Adams, John Quincy, 71
Adams, John, 45, 64
Adams, Thomas, 53
Adolphi, John, 146
Aesculapius, altar of, 7
African Lodge No. 459, EC, 86
Agnew, Spiro T., 154
Ahiman Rexon, 25
Aid and Assist, To (film), 131, 140
Ainslie, Rev. James, 11
Air Force, American, 118, 134
Airforce One, 147
airmail, 124
Alabama State Militia, 181
Alabama, 91
Alabama, Grand Lodge of, 70, 81, 151
Alamogordo, New Mexico, 141
Alaska, Grand Lodge of, 157
Albatross, USS, 96
Albert Pike Lodge No. 177, Kansas, 156
Aldrin, Jr., Edwin E., 148
Alexandria Washington Lodge No. 22, Virginia, 58, 62, 63, 64, 57, 97
Allen E. Roberts Masonic Library and Museum, 181
Allen, Henry, 92
Allen, William, 30
Alnwick Lodge, 13-14
Alsace-Lorraine, Lodge of, Paris, France, 112
America, North, 29
American embassy, Iran, 157
American Expeditionary Force, 118
American Military History, 109
American Union Lodge, 40, 49, 50, 56, 66
American-Canadian Grand Lodge, 155
Anapolis, Maryland, 177
Anchor Communications, 181
Ancient Free Masons (AFM), 34
Ancient Landmarks Lodge No. 319, Indiana, 124

Anderson, Dr. James, 3, 14, 15, 16, 17, 19, 20, 25-26, 37
Anderson, Kenneth L., 80
Anderson, Patrick, 147
Anderson, Robert, 91, 98
André, John, 51
Angerona Lodge No. 168, Tenn., 94
Anglo Saxon Lodge No. 137, New York, 114
Annapolis Basin, Nova Scotia, 29
Annapolis, Lodge at, 36
Annual Assembly and Feast (first), 15-16
Antarctic Continent, 176
Antell, Samuel B., 107
Anthony Lodge No. 200, Kansas, 153
anti-Masonry, 10, 11, 26, 33, 67, 73-77, 81, 89, 111, 136, 155, 157, 159, 161, 162
Antietam, Battle of, 94-95
Antimasonic Party, 75
Antiquity manuscript, 14
Antiquity, Lodge of, 19
Appalachian mountains, 56
Appendant bodies at work during World War II, 131
Apple Tree Tavern, 15, 16
Appomattox, Virginia, 98
Arab Proverb, 176
Archaeologia, 2
Arizona Lodge No. 2, 112, 147
Arizona, Grand Lodge of, 112
Arizona, USS, Memorial, 157-158
Arkansas, 113
Arkansas, Grand Lodge of, 79
Armed Forces, American, 119, 130, 131, 134, 137-138, 177
Armistead, Lewis A., 97, 166
Arms, Grant of, 1
Army of Northern Virginia, Confederate, 98
Arnold, Benedict, 44, 48, 51
Arnold, Gen. Henry H. "Hap", 134, 172
Arthur, Chester Alan, 111
Articles of Association, 53
Articles of Confederation, 53-54, 55

Articles of Union, 27
Ashmole, Elias, 4, 13-14
Athelstan, 3
Atholl Masons, 19
Atholl, Duke of, 26-27
Atichison's Haven, Lodge at, 4
Atlantic Ocean, 126
atom bomb, 129, 141
attacks on Freemasonry, 10-11, 26, 33, 67, 73-77
Auraria, Colorado, 92
Australia, 134
Austria, 117, 140
Austria, Grand Lodge of, 164
Autry, Gene, 125
Aztian Lodge, Arizona, 112
"Baal's Bridge Square", 179
Baldwin, Henry, 71
Balls, John, 106
Baltimore and Ohio Railroad, 79
Baltimore Convention, 79, 81
Baltimore, Maryland, 64, 81
Bank of the United States, 68
Bannock, Montana, 173
Barbary States, 66
Barney, John, 83
Barras, Admiral, 52
Bartholdi, Frederick A., 112
Bartimaeus Lodge, U.D., Indiana, 164
Baruch, Sydney N., 118
Bataan Death March, 134
Batavia, New York, 73-75
Batham, Cyril N., 165 Batt, John, 86
Battle of Bloody March, 32
Bean, James E., 153
Bearly, David, 54
Beauregard, General Pierre Gustave Toutant, 91
Beaver, Fred J. Holt, 112
Beckley, John, 62
Bedford, Jr., Gunning, 54
"Beecher's Bibles", 89
Beery, Wallace, 125
Beginnings of Freemasonry in America, The, 143
Belcher, Johathan, quoted, 29
Bell, John, 90
Belton Lodge No. 155, Texas, 144
Ben Hur, 98, (motion Picture), 125
Bennington, Vermont, 65
Benton Lodge No. 64, Michigan, 138
Benton, Jr., Thomas Hart, 98-99

Berlin, Irving, 124
Beyer, Jean (Jesuit Father), 152
Bible, 5-6, 39, 61, 162, 163, 171
Biddle, Edward, 53
Bill of Rights, 59-60, 62
Bingham, Henry H., 97, 166
Birmingham, Alabama, 123
Biscayne Lodge No. 124, Florida, 135
Bismark Lodge, North Dakota, 113
Bismark, North Dakota, 113
Black, Hugh L., 71
Blackmore, James E., 125
Blair, Jr., John, 52, 54, 58, 71
Blatchford, Daniel, 71
Blue Forget-Me-Not, Masonic Brotherhood of, 69
Bodlin Library, 2
Bonham, James, 80
Booth, Edwin, 102
Booth, John Wilkes, 102
Borgnine, Ernest, 125
Born in Blood: The Lost Secrets of Freemasonry, 9, 73
"Boston Tea Party", 42-43
Boston, Massachusetts, 31, 33, 43, 44, 86
Boswell, John, 6
Botetourt Lodge, Virginia, 36
Bowie, James, 80
Bradley, Omar N. , 144
Breckinridge, Gen. John C., 98
Breed's Hill, 44
Bremen Lodge No. 456, Georgia, 153
Brent, George, 125
Bristol Lodge No. 25, Pennsylvania, 124
British Library, 2
British Museum, 2
British troops, 43, 44, 46, 48, 49, 51-52, 68
Broom, Jacob, 54, 58
Brother Truman, 70, 119, 153
Brotherhood of Man..., *The* (film), 131
Brotherhood, The, 159, 160
Brown, Joe E., 125
Brown, John, 89
Brownson, Nathan, 146
Bryan, William Jennings, 113, 126
Buchanan, James, 88, 89, 90, 105
Buchenwald concentration camp, 133
Buffalo, New York, 115
Builder, The, 80
Builders, The, 80
Bull Run (Manassas), 92

Bullock, Archibald, 146
Bunker Hill, Battle of, 44
Burger, Warren, 154
Burgoyne, John, 48
Burke, Edmund, 43
Burke, Abbot-Bishop George, 166
Burleson, Edward, 80
Burlington, New Jersey, 29
Burma, 133
Burnet, David G., 80
Burton, Harold H., 71
Bush, George Herbert Walker, 162-163
Bushnell, George E., 147
Butler, Benjamin F., 93
Byrd, Admiral Richard E., 126
Byrnes, James F., 71
Cabletow (Philippines), 173
Calhoun, John C., 88
California, 85, 88, 133, 155
California, Grand Lodge of, 79, 85, 147, 158, 163
Camp Floyd, 105
Canada, 44, 52, 146
Canal Zone (Panama), 109, 115
Canterbury Cathedral, 6
Cantor, Eddie, 125
Cantwell's Bridge, Maryland, 37
Capital Lodge No. 110, Iowa, 144
Capitol, U.S., 177
CARE, 140
Carnegy, S.W.B., 83
Carr, Harry, 5, 170
Carroll, Daniel, 53, 54 58
Carson City, Nevada, 101
Carter, James "Jimmy" Earl, 115, 156, 157, 163
Case, James Royal, 53, 152
Cass, Lewis, 67, 79
Caswell, Richard, 53, 146
Catawba Lodge No. 17, North Carolina, 153
Catron, Thomas B., 107
Catton, John, 71
Cedar Rapids, Iowa, 80, 120
Cemetery Ridge, 97
Central Pacific Railroad, 110
Certified Administrative Manager, 181
Cerza, Alphonse, 142
Chamberlain, Gen. Joshua L., 98
Chambersburg, Pennsylvania, 97-98
Champlain, Lake, 48
Charity Lodge No. 190, Pennsylvania, 97

Charles II, 2
Charleston, South Carolina, 32-33, 91
Chaytor, George, 48
Chennault, Gen. Claire, 135
Cherrydale Lodge No. 42, Virginia, 161
Chicago, 138
Chicago, Illinois, 47
Chickahominy River, 94
Child, Dr. William, 95
China, 135
Chittenden, Thomas, 146
Chivington, Rev. John M., 92
Christian, George H., 124
Christiana Ferry, Delaware, 37
Church of England, 159
Church Times, England, 159
Churchill, Winston, 129, 136, 141
Cincinnati, Society of the, 58
City Gazette, Charlotte, South Carolina, 62
Civil War, American, ix, 86, 89-90, 91-99, 105, 111, 162, 113, 125, 138
Civilian Conservation Corps, 181
Clark Air Force Base, 153
Clark, Gen. Mark Wayne, 135
Clark, George Rogers, 49, 65, 66
Clark, Thomas C., 71
Clark, William, 112
Clark, William, 66
Clarke, John C., 80
Clarke, John H., 71
Claudy, Carl H., 123, 130, 137
Clausen, Henry C., quoted 65; 125
Clay, Henry, 67, 71, 79-80, 88, 90
Clemens, Samuel L. (Mark Twain), 101
Cleveland, Ohio, 78
Clinton, DeWitt, 60, 69
Clinton, George, 60
Coats, John, 37
Coburn, Charles, 125
Cody, William F. "Buffalo Bill", 125, 162
Cohan, George M., 124
Coil's Masonic Encyclopedia, 146-147, 155
Coil, Henry Wilson, 3, 146, 155
colleges and Freemasonry, 178
Colorado, 109
Colorado, Grand Lodge of, 92, 97, 163
Colorado, Territory of, 92
Columbia Lodge No. 30, 110
Columbia, South Carolina, 131
Comacine Masters, 3

Committee of the Whole, 57-58
compromises, 79-80, 88, 90
CompuServe, 165
computers and Freemasonry, 179
concentration camps (German), 127
concentration camps, 133
Concord Lodge No. 688, Ohio, 145
Concordia Lodge No. 50, South Carolina, 144
Confederate States of America, 91, 102, 103, 111
Congress of the United States, 64, 66, 67, 80, 103, 104, 115, 118, 129, 132, 145, 156, 162
Congress, Continental, 41, 44, 45, 47, 49, 51, 53, 54, 55, 56, 59
Connecticut Masonic Research Lodge, 152
Connecticut, 40, 53, 59, 60, 65
Connecticut, Grand Lodge of, 40, 86, 152, 163
"Conservators of Sumbolic Masonry", 95
Constitution of the United States, 54, 59, 60, 61, 104, 160
Constitution (frigate), 64
Constitutional Convention, 42, 55, 56-57, 59, 117
Constitutions of 1738, 26
Constitutions of Freemasonry, 14, 15, 17, 19-20; abbreviated, 20-24, 25, 26, 37
Constitutions of the Antients, 25
"Constitutions, Book of" (Preston's), 19
Cook, Levi, 67
Cooke Manauscript, 3, 5, 14
Cooke, Alistair, 127
Coolidge, Calvin, 124, 125
corner stones, 62, 63, 79, 88, 111, 123, 145, 148, 177
Cornerstone Computer Chapter (Philalethes), 165
Cornwallis, Lord, 47, 52
Court of Appeals, 160
cowan, 7-8
Cowper, William, 17
Coxe, Daniel, 30
Craik, Dr. James, 64
"Crisis, The", 46
Crittenden, John J., 91
Cross, Col. Edward E., x, 94, 95
Crown Ale House, 15
Cryptic Masons, General Grand Council of, 157-158

Cryptic Masons, Grand Council of, Iowa, 165
Cuba, 114
Culdees, 3
Cunningham, John D., 137
Cushing, William, 60, 71
Czolgosz, Leon (assassin), 115
"Daisy Girl", 147
Dakota Territory, 106, 112
Dakota, Grand Lodge of, 113
Dane, Doyle, 147
Darrow, Clarence, 125-126
Daugherty, Henry M., 123
David, King, 5
Davis, Jefferson, 91
Davis, John W., 125 Dayton, Elias, 52
de Grasse, 51-52
Decatur, Jr., Stephen, 68-69
Declaration of Independence, 45-46, 52-53
DeFore, Dan, 125
Delaware River, 46-47
Delaware, 37, 45, 54, 59
Delaware, Grand Lodge of, 37, 48, 66
DeMille, Cecil B., 125
DeMolay, Order of, 154
Denslow, Ray V., 70, 146
Denslow, William R., 70, 91, 146
Denver Lodge No. 5, Colorado, 97
depression (Great), 127
Dermott, Laurence, 24-25
Desaguliers, Dr. John Theophilus, 3, 16
Dewey, Commodore George, 114
Dewey, Thomas E., 144
Dick, Dr. Elisha Cullen, 62, 64
Dickenson, Alharon, 80
Dickinson, John, 53, 54, 58
Dinwiddie Union Lodge No. 23, VA, 92
Diocletian, Emperor, 6-7
Dirkson, Everett M., 151
Disney, Roy, 125
District of Columbia, 68, 91, 165, 171
District of Columbia, Grand Lodge of, 67, 88, 90, 158, 161, 177
Documents Illustrative of the Formation of the Union of the American States, 42, 57
Doenitz, Adm. Karl, 138
Dole, Robert, 156-157
Doolittle, James H. "Jimmy", 134, 172
Door of Virtue Lodge No. 111, Missouri, 66, 112

Dorchester Lodge, Vermont, 65
Dorchester (U.S. troop ship), 136
Douglas, Stephen A., 88, 90
Douglas, William O., 71
Dove, John, 71, 81, 83, 86
Dover, Delaware, 37
Downen, Robert L., 156-157
draft act, 132
draft, 95-96
Drake, Francis, 18
Drummond, Josiah Hayden, 31, 70
dry-diker, 8
Dublin, University of, 4-5,
Dunckerly, Thomas, 25
Dunmore, Lord John Murray, 43
Duportail, Louis le Begue, 52
Dustin, F. G., 176
Duvall Lodge No. 6, Kentucky, 153
Early Masonic Catechisms, 8
Eastern Airlines, 119
Edinburgh, Lodge at, 6, 7, 8
Edon, Lieutenant, 95
Edson, Merritt, 135 Egypt, 6
Eiffel Tower Masonic Club, 139
Eisenhower, Dwight D., 163, 177
Ellery, William, 53
Elliott, Bernard, 33
Ellsworth, Oliver, 60, 71
England, (Great Britain), 1, 4, 9, 14, 38, 41, 43, 44-45, 67, 127, 130, 165
England, Grand Lodge of (Antients), 18, 19, 24, 26, 37
England, Grand Lodge of (Moderns), 15; 15-16, 17, 18, 19, 26, 30, 32, 33, 34, 36, 40, 41, 56. 86
England, Grand Lodge of All, 18
England, Grand Lodge of, South of the River Trent, 18
England, United Grand Lodge of, 1, 4, 35, 160
Enola Gay (B-29 bomber), 141
Ervin, Jr., Samuel J., 153
Essenes, 3
Euclid,.11
Europe, 117, 130, 135, 138, 140, 142, 144
Excelsior Lodge No. 60, 160
exclusive jurisdication, 17
Fairbanks, Douglas, 125
Fairfax Lodge No. 43, Virginia, 60
Falmouth Lodge, Virginia, 36
"Farewell Address", Washington's, 63-64
Farmer's Lodge No. 20, Ohio, 60

Farragut, Admiral David G., 93, 178
Fascists, 136
Fay, Bernard, 132
Fayette Lodge No. 107, Ohio, 123
Federal Bureau of Investigation, 147
Federal Lodge No. 1, D.C., 123, 147
Feliciana Lodge No. 31, Louisiana, 96
Ferdinand, Archduke Francis, 117
Field, Stephen J., 71
5th Army, 135
Fifth Fleet (in Pacific), 135
5th New Hampshire Regiment, 94, 95
Fillmore, Millard, 88
Fire of London, The Great, 9-10
First Lodge, Boston, Massachusetts, 31, 53
Fitch, John, 124
Fletcher, Richard E., xi
Florida, 122
Florida, Grand Lodge of, 79
"Flying Tigers", 135
footnotes, ix, x-xi
Ford, Gerald R., 147, 154, 155
Ford, Henry, 124
Forrest, Gen. Nathan Bedford, 94
Fort Hamar, 56
Fort Niagara, 74
Fort Stanwix, 48
Fort Sumter, 91, 98
Fortitude Lodge No. 107, Kansas, 127
46th Foot (British), 51
Fosdick, Raymond B., 120
Fountain Lodge No. 60, Indiana, 125
Four Chaplains, 136-137
Four Chaplains, Chapel of, 137
Four Crowned Martyrs, 6-7
14th Air Force, 135
Fox, George, 136
France, 48, 51, 64, 112, 119, 120, 132, 133, 1366, 137, 165
France, Grand Lodge National, 157
France, Grand Lodge of, 137
Franco, Francisco, 157
Franklin D. Roosevelt Lodge, Paris, France, 137
Franklin, Benjamin, 30, 31, 37, 45, 47, 48, 53, 57, 58, 59
Fraysee, Pierre, 136
Frazier, Simon, 36
Fredericksburg Lodge, No.4, Virginia, 35-36, 44, 58, 61
Fredericksburg, Battle of, x

Freemasonry Dissected, 175
Freemasonry in American History, 75
Freemasonry in the Thirteen Colonies, 80, 130
Freemasonry's Servant, 120
Freemasons' Hall, London, England, 27, 160
French fleet, 51-52
French troops, 48, 51-52
Fulton, Missouri, 141
"Funniest Language", 169
Galveston, Texas, 96
Garfield, James A., 110, 111
Gaspee, 43
Gates, Horatio, 48, 51
Gaunt, Rev. Eric E., quoted 159
Geary, John W., 89-90
General Grand Lodge, 84, 121
General Grand Master, 49-50
"General", the (train), 92
George C. Whiting Lodge No. 22, D.C., 135
George II, 2
George VI, King of England, (Alfred Frederick Arthur George), 136
George Washington Masonic National Memorial, 115, 155, Presidential plagues in, 155; description of, 156
Georgia, 146
Georgia, 32, 58, 59, 92, 146
Georgia, Grand Lodge of, 32, 56
Germany, 117, 126, 127, 130
Gettysburg, Battle of, xi, 96-97, 105
Gettysburg, Pennsylvania, 166
Gibson, Hoot, 125
Gilman, Charles, 85
Girard, Stephen, 68
Glasgow, Lodge of, 6
Glenn, Jr., John H., 145
Gloucester, Virginia, 36
Glover, John, 47
Goethals, George W., 109
Goldwater, Barry, 147-148
Goose and Gridiron Ale-house, 15, 16
Gothic Manuscripts (Constitutions), 5, 7, 11, 12, 17
Gould, Robert Freke, quoted, 1; 3, 4, 6-7, 10, 17, 24, 31, 51
Gourgas medal, 143
Gourgas, John J., 143
Government Printing Office, 42
Grand Army of the Republic (GAR), 138

Grand Design, The, ix
Grand Lodge of England North of the River Trent, 19
Grand Lodge of Scotland Year Book, The, 1, 4, 6, 8
Grand Lodge of the Most Ancient and Honorable Society of Free and Accepted Masons for the State of Rhode Island and Providence Plantations, 40 (see Rhode Island, Grand Lodge of)
Grand Lodge (England), 1, 4, 6, 10, 11, 15, 16, 17, 32, 35
Grand Lodge manuscript, 11, 14
Grand Masters, Conference of, 122
Grand Secretaries, Conference of, 122
Grandview Lodge No. 618, Missouri, 119
Grant, Gen. Ulyses S., 98, 110
"Grapevine Bridge", 94
Green Dragon Tavern, 42
Greene, Nathaniel, 47, 49, 51
Greeneville Lodge No. 119, Tennessee, 102
Greeneville No. 119, 105
Gridley, Jeremy, 40
Gridley, Richard, 50
Grissom, Virgil I., 148
Guildhall, London, 1, 15
Guiteau, Charles J., 111
Gutenberg (Johannes Gensfleisch zur Laden), 171
Hahn, Conrad, 151-152
Halliwell, J.O. (also Halliwell-Philips), 2
Hamilton, Alexander, 61
Hamilton, Henry, 49
Hancock, Gen. Winfield S., 97
Hancock, John, 53, 54, 59, 146
Hannah (schooner), 43
Hanover Lodge, North Carolina, 53
Hanson, Vee, 81
Harasim, Paul, 166
Harding, Warren G., 123, 123-124, 163
Harlan, John M., 71
Harmony Lodge No. 6, Texas, 96
Harnett, Cornelius, 53
Harper's Ferry, 89
Harper, Pennye, 179
Harriet Lane, USS, 96
Harrison's Landing, Virginia, 93-94
Harrison, William Henry, 67
Harry S. Truman Library, 153
Hart, John E., 96

Hart, Peter, 98
Hawaii, Grand Lodge of, 158, 163
Haywood, Harry Leroy, 80, 113
Hearst, Randolph, 114
Heart, Jonathan, 50, 52, 56
Heaton, Ronald, 53, 71, 152
Henry, Patrick, 43, 49, 60
Herman Lodge No. 6, West Virginia, 125
Herndon, Edward, 83
Heth, Gen. Henry, 96, 105
Hewes, Joseph, 53
Hiram Lodge in New Haven, Connecticut, 40
Hilton, James, 135
Hiram Lodge No. 1, Conn., 44
Hiram Lodge No. 10, D.C., 124
Hiroshima, Japan, 141
History of Freemasonry, The, 4
History of the Fifth Regiment, New Hampshire Volunteers, x
Hitler, Adolph, 127, 129, 138, 140, 155
hoax, 174-175
Hoban, James, 63
Holland Lodge No. 8, New York, 127
Hollenbeck Lodge No.319, California,134
Hollywood, California, 124, 131, 140
Holme, Randle, 14
Holy Saint Johns, Lodge of, 170-171
Hooker, Gen. Joseph, x
Hooper, William, 53
Hoover, J. Edgar, 123, 147
Hope Lodge No. 244, New York, 153
Hornet, USS, 135
Hospital Visitation Program (Veterans), 137, 139, 140
House of Representatives, 59
House Undivided, ix
Houston Post, The, 166
Houston, Sam, 79
Howard, John Edgar, 146
Hudson Lodge No. 68, Ohio, 89
Hughan, W. J., quoted, 13
Hughes Army Lodge, 94
Hughes, Col. Edward E., 94
Humphreys, Charles, 53
Hungary, Grand Lodge of, 163-164
Hunt, Charles C., 80
Idaho, Grand Lodge of, 163
Illinois, 160
Illinois, Grand Lodge of, 79
Illustrations of Masonry, 78
Imagination Unlimited!, 131

Impeachment (of Andrew Johnson) results, 104
Imperia, Italy (prison camp), 136
Independence Hall, 45
Independence Rock, Wyoming, 106
Independence, Missouri, 152-153
Indian Territory, Grand Lodge of, 113
Indiana, Grand Lodge of, 69, 164, 167
Indianapolis Star, The, 164
Indians, 48, 67, 90, 101, 113, 114
Iowa Masonic Library, 80
Iowa Research Lodge No. 2, 164
Iowa, 161
Iowa, Grand Lodge of, 80, 98, 120
Iran, 157
Ireland, 4
Ireland, Grand Lodge of, 4, 24, 65
"iron curtain", 141
"Islamic Resistance Movement-Palestine", 161-162
Islamic World Congress, 155
Isreal, Grand Lodge of, 145
Italy, 126, 135
Jachin and Boaz, 78
Jacinto, Battle of, 80
Jackson, Andrew, 67, 68, 71, 79, 80
Jackson, Dr. Charles T., 29
Jackson, General Thomas "Stonewall", 93
Jackson, Rev. Jesse, 160
Jackson, Robert H., 71
James River, 98
James Royal Case Medal of Excellence, 151, 152
James VI, King, 4
James VI, King, Scotland, 179
Japan, 115, 118, 122, 126, 133, 136, 141, 144
Japan, Grand Lodge of, 174
Japanese prison camp, 133
Jay, John, 63
Jefferson, Thomas, 45, 46, 66
Jesuits (Society of Jesus), 133, 152
John, 2nd Duke of Montague, 16-17
John, Duke of Atholl, 39
Johns, John, 4
Johnson, Andrew, 102-105
Johnson, Andrew, 89
Johnson, Harold K., 134
Johnson, Lyndon B., 134, 147, 151, 153
Johnson, Melvin Maynard, 31, 86, 142-143

193

Johnston, Samuel "Sam", 35, 60
Jolson, Al (Asa Yoelson), 124
Jones, Anson, 79, 80
Jones, John Paul, 177
Joppa Lodge No. 346, Maryland, 36
Justice, Department of, 123
Kane Lodge No. 454, New York, 126, 144
Kansas, Grand Lodge of, 89, 173
Kaskaskia, 49
Kellog, Frank B., 126
"Kellog-Briand Pact", 126
Kelso, 6
Kemper, James L., 97
Kennedy, Edward M. "Ted", 160
Kennedy, John F., 147
Kent, Duke of, 27
Kentucky, 90, 104
Kentucky, Grand Chapter of (RAM), 79
Kentucky, Grand Lodge of, 65-66, 67
Key to Freemasonry's Growth, 20
Keystone Lodge No. 243, Missouri, 126
Khomeini, Ayatollah Ruhollah, 157
Kilwinning Lodge No. 297, Michigan, 119
Kilwinning Lodge No. 356, Ohio, 115
Kilwinning, Lodge of, 6, 7, 8, 36
King, Adm. Ernest J., 135
King, Rufus, 54, 58
Knights Templar, 91, 124
Knight, Stephen, 159, 160
Knight, Stephen, 73
Knights of Columbus, 119, 120
Knox, Henry, 47, 52, 58, 63
Kosciuzko Lodge, New York, 47
Korea, 144
Korea, South, 177
Kosciuzko, Thaddeus, 47
Ku Klux Klan, 94
Lacy, Roger, 32
Lafayette Lodge No. 23, Georgia, 91
Lafayette, Marquis de, 48, 51-52, 52, 71
LaFollette, Robert M., 125
Lake, Simon, 124
Lamar, Joseph R., 71
Lamar, Mirabeau B., 80
Lancaster Lodge No. 54, Nebraska, 148
"Land Ordinance", 56
landmarks, 24, 26, 81, 152
Landon, Alfred H., 127
Landrum, J.D., quoted, 101
Langston, LaMoine, 106
Lanier, Dixon, 170

LaRouche, Lyndon, 165
Laurens, Henry, 53, 54, 146
League City Lodge No. 1053, Texas, 135
Leake, W.W., 96
Lee, Gen. Charles, 46
Lee, General Robert E., 92, 93, 94, 98
Lee, Richard Henry, 45
Lehy, Patrick, 160
LeRoy, New York, 73
Letters of a Self-Made Diplomat to His President, 126
Lewis, Meriweather, 66, 112
Lexington Lodge No. 1, Kentucky, 65, 91
"Liber A", 30
"Liber B", 30
Liberia, 159
Liberty Bell, 110
Liberty Island, 111
Library and Museum of Our National Heritage, 154
Limerick No. 13, Lodge of, Ireland, 179
limerick, 170
Lincoln Lodge No. 19, Nebraska, 118, 126
Lincoln, Abraham, x, 88, 90, 91, 92, 93, 94, 102
Lincoln, Benjamin, 48, 52
Lindbergh, Charles A., 126, 134
Linn Banks Lodge No. 126, 97
Lions, 162
Lippman, Jr., Theo, ix
Little Masonic Library, 20
Little Rock, Arkansas, 99
Little, Brown (publishers), 132
Livingston, Robert R., 39, 45, 61, 66
Lloyd, Harold, 125
Lodge No. 14, Dela, 58
Lodge No. 16, Maryland, 58
Lodge No. 18, Dela, 58
Lodge No. 227, I.C., 51
Logan, Gen. John A., 138
London Masons Company, 10
London, England, 1, 9-10, 14, 17, 18, 170
Longworth, Henry Wadsworth, 45
Lookout Mountain, Colorado, 125
Lost Horizon, 135
Louisiana Territory, 66
Louisiana, Grand Lodge of, 68, 80, 96
Loyalty Lodge No. 529, California, 125
MacArthur, Douglas, 134, 139, 141, 145, 172

Mackey, Albert, 24, 33
Macoy Publishing and Masonic Supply Co., Inc., 80, 81, 122, 147
Madison Lodge No. 5, Wisconsin, 125
Madison, Dolly, 68
Magnolia Lodge No. 20, Ohio, 110
Magruder, Gen., 96
Maine, 127
Maine, Grand Lodge of, 70, 75
Maine, USS, 114
Mainwaring, Col. Henry, 4
Maira, Earl of, 26
Malta ld, 154
Malta Lodge No. 465, Michigan, 147
Man Called Intrepid, A, 129
Marietta, Ohio, 40, 50, 56
Marine Band, United States, 124
Marion Lodge No. 70, Ohio, 123
Marquis Who's Who, 181
Marsengill, Jerald "Jerry" E., 80, 164-165
Marshall Islands, 135
Marshall, George C., 132-133, 144
Marshall, John, 60, 64, 71, 79
Marshall, Thurgood, 72
Martin, Alexander, 146
Mary Land, Lodge at, 36
Mary's Chapel, Lodge of, 6
Maryland, 53, 54, 60, 67, 94, 146
Maryland, Grand Lodge of, 37, 56, 63, 79
Mason Regulations, code of, 1
Masonic Brotherhood of the Blue Forget-Me-Not, The, 130, 165
"Masonic cigarettes", 132
"Masonic Lodge, structure of", 171-172
Masonic Membership of the Founding Fathers, 53
Masonic Service Association, The, xi, 53, 80, 84, 117, 120, 121,,122, 129, 130, 131, 132, 137, 139, 140, 152, 181
Masonic Service Centers, 131, 139
Masonic Sketches, 13
Masonry Dissected, 38, 78
Masons Who Helped Shape Our Nation, 65, 125
Masons' Company, London, 1
Masons' Hall, London, 1, 13
Masons' Hall, Richmond, Virginia, 34, 71, 98, 148-149
Massachusetts Convention, 59
Massachusetts, 29, 30, 31, 47, 53, 54, 65, 70, 146

Massachusetts, Grand Lodge of, 8, 86, 143
Massachusetts, Provincial Grand Lodge of, 36, 50
Master's Lodge, Massachusetts, 31
Masters' Lodge, Rhode Island, 40
Masters' Lodge, South Carolina, 33
Mathews, Stanley, 71
Matinecock Lodge No. 806, Oyster Bay, New York, 115
May, Thomas F., viii
Mayer, Louis B., 125
McCarthy, Charles, 75
McClellan, General George B., x, 92, 93, 94
McDowell, 93
McHenry, James, 54, 58
McKinley, William, 95, 101-102, 113, 114, 115
McLaughlin, W. Hugh, 153
McLeod, Wallace, vii-vii, ix, xi, 8, 29
Mechanicsville, Virginia, 93-94
Melrose St. John, Lodge of, 8
Memorial Day (Decoration Day), 138
Mercer, Hugh, 47
Merchants Lodge No. 277, Quebec, 53
Merrick, Gordon, 15
Mexico, 70, 79, 80, 89, 118, 163
Mexico, Grand Lodge of, 70
Michigan City Lodge No. 47, California, 110
Michigan, Grand Lodge of, 67, 75, 79, 81
Minnesota, Grand Lodge of, 88, 113, 163
Minton, Sherman, 71-72
Mississippi River, 49, 56, 93
Mississippi, 122
Mississippi, Grand Lodge of, 69, 95
Missouri Military Lodge, 106
Missouri River, 66
Missouri, 164
Missouri, Grand Lodge of, 70, 86, 105, 106, 118, 153
Missouri, USS, 141
Mitscher, Adm. Marc A., 135
Mix, Tom, 125
Mock Masonry, 33
Moira, Earl of, 26
Monitor, Webb's, 79
Monmouth Lodge No. 172, New Jersey,124
"Monroe Doctrine", 71
Monroe, James, 66, 71

Montagu, John Duke of, 26
Montague, Paul J., 153
Montana State Patrol, 174
Montana, 173
Montgomery, Gen. Richard, 44
Montgromerie Arms Tavern, New York, 39
Montreal, 44
Moody, William H., 72
Moore, Charles W., 83
Moose River Lodge No.82, Vermont, 136
Moral Duties, Manuscript of, 2
Moray, Robert, 4
"Morgan Affair", 73-75
Morgan, General Daniel, 48, 51
Morgan, William, 73-75
Morgan, William, monument to, 74-75
Mormons (Latter Day Saints), 79-80, 106
Morris, Rob, 95
Morris, Robert, 57
Morristown, New Jersey, 46, 47, 50
Morton, Jacob, 61
Mother Kilwinning, 8
Mount Vernon, 61, 64
motion pictures (for MSA), 122
Moyers, Bill D., 147
Mt. Moriah Lodge No. 15, Carson City, 109
Muhlenberg, Frederick Augustus, 62
Muhlenberg, John P.G., 52
Mystic Tie Lodge No. 308, Indiana, 135
Nagasaki, Japan, 141
National Masonic Convention, 81
Nauvoo, Illinois, 79
Naval Lodge No. 2012, England, 136
Navy Academy, 177
Navy, U.S., 181
Nazism, 127, 130, 136, 140
Nebraska, Grand Lodge of, 90, 163
Nelson, Samuel, 72
Nelson, Thomas, 146
Nevada, 101
New England, 69, 79
New Hampshire, 54, 60, 115, 146, 178
New Hampshire, Grand Lodge of, 40-41, 46, 85, 94
New Jersey, 30, 53, 54, 91
New Jersey, Grand Lodge of, 56
New Mexico, 141
New Mexico, Grand Lodge of, 107
New Orleans, 68, 93
New York Gazette, 38-39

New York Lodge No. 350, 102
New York militia, 67
New York Stock Exchange, 127
New York Times, The, 126, 132
New York, 30, 37, 38, 52, 60, 69, 80, 81, 110, 111, 164
New York, Grand Lodge of, 39-40, 56, 61, 70, 75, 80, 81, 120
New, Harry S., 124
Newman, Robert, 44
Newport, Rhode Island, 40
Newton, Joseph Fort (D.D.), 80, quoted 87, 151; 122
Niagara River, 67
Nine Sisters, Lodge of, 177
Nixon, Richard M., 153, 154
Nobel Peace Prize, 115, 126
Norfolk, Duke of, 30
North Africa, 66
North Carolina, 34, 53, 60-61, 80, 146
North Carolina, Grand Lodge of, 35, 60
North Church, Old, Mass., 43
North Dakota, Grand Lodge of, 112, 113,163
North Korea, 151
North Pole, 126
North Star Lodge No. 8, New Hampshire, 94
Northern Light, The, 167
Notre Dame, University of, 152
Nova Scotia, 29
O'Brien, Dr. John A., 152
Oglethorpe, James Edward, 32
Ohio River, 56
Ohio Territory, 56
Ohio, Grand Chapter of (RAM), 79
Ohio, Grand Lodge of, 40, 50, 56, 66, 67, 79, 115, 145
Okinawa, Battle of, 141
Oklahoma, Grand Lodge of, 113
Old Charges, 8
Old Elmwood Cemetery, Batavia, 74
Olive Branch Lodge No. 64, Vermont, 135
Olympic Games (1984), 158
Ontario, Canada, 74
operative masons, 6
Oregon, 85-86
Oregon, Grand Lodge of, 79, 90
Oriental Lodge No. 240, Michigan, 123
Oxford University, 2
Oxnard, Thomas, 36, 40

196

Pacific Ocean, 66, 138
"Pact of Paris", 126
Pahlevi, Shah Mohammed Reza, 157
Paine, Robert Treat, 53
Paine, Thomas, quoted, 46
Palistine Lodge No. 357, Michigan, 124
Panama Canal, 115, 156
Paris, France, 126, 139, 177
Parsons, Samuel H., 50 Parvin,
    Theodore S., 80
Paterson, William, 54, 58, 72
Pawtucket, Rhode Island, 181
Payne, George, 16, 21-22
Peabody, James H., 109
Peale, D.D., Norman Vincent, 161
Pearl Harbor, Hawaii, 133, 181
Pekin Lodge No. 29, Illinois, 151
penalties, 9
Pendleton, Edmund, 60
Pennsylvania Gazette, 30
Pennsylvania, 30, 44-45, 46, 49, 53, 54,
    59, 89, 103
Pennsylvania, Grand Lodge of, 37, 50, 56,
    78, 89, 97, 166
Pennsylvania, Provincial Grand Lodge
    of, 66
Pentalpha Lodge No. 23, D.C., 110
Pershing, Gen. John J. "Black Jack", 118
Persian Gulf action, 155
Petersburg Lodge No. 15, Virginia, 97
Philadelphia, 33, 41, 45, 46, 49, 110,
    117, 147
Philalethes Society, The, 53, 69, 71, 122,
    136, 141-142, 146, 151,152, 156, 161,
    165, 166
Philalethes, The, 80, 142, 146, 148, 152,
    156, 169-170, 173
Philanthropic Lodge, Mass, 47
Philanthropy Lodge No. 235, 89
Philippine Islands, 118, 134, 136, 139,
    140, 153
Philippines, Grand Lodge of, 136, 174
Phoenix, Arizona, 112
Pickett, Gen. George E., 97
Pierce, William, 58
Pike, Albert (statue of), 165
Pike, Albert, 99
Pitney, Mahlon, 72
plague, the great, 9
Plater, George, 60
Platte Valley Lodge No. 32, Nebraska,
    125, 162

Poinsett, Joel R., 69-70, 163
poinsettia, 70
Poland, 47
Polar Star Lodge No. 90, Missouri, 101
Pollack, Melvin, 153
Pope, Gen. x
Port Royal Kilwinning Crosse Lodge
    No. 2, Virginia, 8, 36
Port Royal, Nova Scotia, 29
Port Washington, Wisconsin, 96
Post, Wiley, 126
Pound, Roscoe, 148
Preble, Commodore Edward, 66
President of the United States, 59, 61,
    62, 103, 110, 114, 137, 140, 141, 143,
    147, 153, 154, 157, 162, 183
President's House (White House), 62, 68
President's Men, The, 147
Preston, William, 19, 69, 78
Price, Henry, 31
Prichard, Samuel, 38, 78
Prince Hall Masonry, 86, 147, 159, 160,
    163, 164, 165, 166
Prince, H.M.S., 25
Provincial Grand Master, 31
Provincial Grand Master, South
    Carolina, 33
Pueblo, USS, 151
Pulaski Lodge, Ill., 47
Pulaski, Count Casimir, 47
Pulaskia Lodge, Ver., 47
Pullman, George, 112
Pusan Masonic Club, Korea, 177
Putnam Lodge, Massachusetts, 98
Putnam, Rufus, 56, 66
pyramids, 6
Quatuor Coronati Lodge No. 2076,
    England, 4, 6-7, 165
Quebec, 44, 65
Quincke, Walter F., 142
Randall, Andrew, 123
Randolph, Edmund, 57, 58, 59, 60, 62
Randolph, Peyteon, 41, 53, 54
Ratoff, Gregory, 146
Rauschnigg, Hermann, 155
Reagan, Ronald Wilson, 157, 161
Recovery Lodge No. 31, SC, 163
Reed, Stanley F., 72
Regius Manuscript (also Poem), 1, 2, 3, 7,
    14, 180
Renovation Lodge No. 97, New York, 112
Revere, Paul, 43, 44

Revolution and Freemasonry, 132
Rhode Island, 40, 43, 47, 53, 61, 78. 79
Richmond Chapter No. 3, RAM, Virginia, 149
Richmond Randolph Lodge No. 19, Virginia, 149
Richmond, Virginia, 43, 81, 93, 138, 161
Rickenbacker, Eddie, 119
ritual, Masonic, 10, 11-12, 16, 82, 83, 95
River of Years, 87
Riverside Lodge No. 635, California, 155
Roberdeau, Daniel, 53
Roberts, Allen E., vii, viii, ix-xi, 152, 181
Roberts, Kenneth, 48
Robey, Donald M., 161
Robinson, John C., 105
Robinson, John J., 9, quoted, 73
Rochambeau, 51-52
Rochester Lodge No. 21, New York, 126
Rocky Mountain Lodge No. 205, Utah, 96, 105
Rocky Mountains, Colorado, 92
Rodney, Caeser, 45
Rogers, Roy, 125
Rogers, William Penn Adair (Will Rogers), 125, 126
Roman College of Artificers, 3
Rome, University of, 152
Roosevelt, Eleanor, 137
Roosevelt, Franklin Delano, 127, 129,137
Roosevelt, Theodore, 114, 115, 118, 177
Root, Elihu, 177
Ross, Marion A., 93 Rowe, John, 50
Rotary, 162
Rough Riders, 114
Roxbury, Mass., 50
Royal Arch Lodge No. 4, Penns., 68
Royal Arch Mason, 80, 146, 165
Royal Arch Masonry, 25, 36, 70, 73-74, 79, 165
Royal Arch Masons, International, General Grand Chapter of, 14-15, 69, 79
Royal Canadian Mounted Police, 176-177
Royal Exchange Lodge, Norfolk, Virginia, 35
Royal Library, 2
Royal Navy Lodge No. 429, England, 4
Royal Navy, 25
Royal Society, England, 16
Royal White Hart Lodge, North Carolina, 34, 148-149
Rummer and Grapes Tavern, 15

Russell Lodge No. 177, Kansas, 156
Russell, Richard B., 147
Russia, 115
Rutledge, Wiley B., 72
Saga of the Holy Royal Arch of Freemasonry, The, 15
San Francisco, Calif., 85, 110
San Juan Hill, Cuba, 114
Santa Anna, 80
Santo Domingo, 51
Saratoga, 48
Saudi Arabia, 155
Savannah, Georgia, 89
Savannah, Lodge at, 32
Sayer, Antony, (first Grand Master), 16
Scala, Charles, 63
Schaw Statutes, 4, 7, 8, 179
Schirra, Jr., Walter M., 148
Schley, Winfield Scott, 93
Schoonover, George L., 80, 120
Schuyler, Gen, Philip, 48
Scoon and Perth, Lodge, 4
"Scopes Trial", 125-126
Scopes, John T., 125-126
Scotland, 4, 7, 8, 29, 177
Scotland, Grand Lodge of, 8, 24, 26, 36, 56, 145
Scotland, Grand Master Mason, 136
Scott, General Winfield, 80, 91
Scottish Rite, 161
Scottish Rite, NMJ, 143, 154, 167
Scottish Rite, SJ, 134, 166, 172
Scudder, Townsend, 120
Second Lodge in Boston, 31
secrecy, 10, 41, 42, 45, 57, 75-76, 167
Secret Journals of the Acts and Proceedings of U.S. Congress, 42
Seekers of Truth, 132, 156, 161, 168,169
Sentelle, Judge David Bryan, 160-161
Seven Days Battle, 93-94, 181
17th British Regiment, 50
Shakespeare, William, 162
"Shangrila", 135
Shawnees, 67
Sherman, John, 110
Sherman, Roger, 45
Shiloh Lodge, North Dakota, 113
Short Talk Bulletins, 122
Shrine, 161
Sibley, Gen. H.H., 112
Singleton, Jerry, 153
Skelton, Richard B. "Red", 167

Skene, John, 29
Smith, Dwight L., 69, 152
Smith, Jonathan Baynard, 53
Sojourners Lodge, Panama, 156-157
Solomon Lodge, Arizona, 112
Solomon's Lodge No. 1, Georgia, 32, 53
Solomon's Lodge No. 1, South Carolina, 163
Solomon's Lodge, South Carolina, 33
Solomon's Temple, King, 5, 11
Solomon, King, 3
Sousa, John Philip, 124
South Carolina Gazette, 32-33
South Carolina, 146
South Carolina, 32, 45, 54, 70, 80, 88
South Carolina, Grand Lodge of, 34, 56, 131
South Dakota, Grand Lodge of, 113
South Pacific, 135
Southern Baptist Convention, 78, 166
Soviet Union, 141
space program, 145, 148
Spain, 114, 157
Spain, Grand Lodge of, 157
Speculative Masons, 6
Spirit of St. Louis, The, 126
Spiritual Lodge No. 16, Maryland, 58
Springfield Lodge No. 4, Illinois, 88
St. Andrew's, Mass, 42, 44, 48, 53, 60, 66, 178
St. Bernard's Lodge No. 122, Scotland, 177
St. Clair, Arthur, 52, 54
St. Francisville, Louisiana, 96
St. Giles, Edinburgh, 6
St. Jean d'Ecosse du Contrat Social, Lodge of, 48
St. John the Baptist Research Lodge, Nebraska, 166
St. John's Church, Virginia, 43
St. John's Lodge No. 1, New York, 39 61, 163
St. John's Lodge, Massachusetts, 29, 44, 58
St. John's Lodge, New Hampshire, 53, 178
St. John's Lodge, New Jersey, 60
St. John's Lodge, Pennsylvania, 53
St. John's Lodge, Princeton, 53
St. John's Lodge, Rhode Island, 40
St. John's Lodge, Yankton, Dakota Ter., 106

St. John's Provincial Grand Lodge of Massachusetts, 40 St. Joseph, Missouri, 86
St. Louis Lodge No. 111, 112
St. Louis, Missouri, 49
St. Nicholas, Church of, 6
St. Paul's Cathedral, 3
Stafford, Thomas P., 148
Stanford, Leland, 110
Star of the East Lodge No. 640, Japan, 144
Stationers' Hall, England, 26
Statue of Liberty, 111, 112
Statues of Freemasons in District of Columbia, 154
Statutes of Laborers, 9
Stephenson, Sir William, 129
Stevens, A.H., 98
Stevens, Thaddeus, 103
Stevenson, William, 129
Stewart, Potter, 72
Stillwell, Gen. Joseph W. "Vinegar", 134
Stockton, Richard, 53
Stockwell, Walter William, quoted 117
stone masons, 5-6
Stony Point, New York, 50
Storey, Captain Edward Faris, 101
Stowe, Harriet Beecher, 88
Sts. John Days, 18
Sts. John, Festival of, 49, 50
Studholme Lodge No. 1591, England, 136
Sullivan, John, 40, 46, 53, 146
Sun, Grand Lodge of the, (Germany), 130
Supreme Court, United States, 63, 71, 79, 115, 133, 147, 154
Sutter's Mill, Calif., 85
Swayne, Noah H., 72
Swiss Grand Lodge Alpina, 136
Switzerland, 136
symbolism, 178
Taft, William Howard, 115
Tarawa, 135
Tarrytown, New York, 51
Task Force 58, 135
Tatsch, Jacob Hugo, 80, 81, 130
taverns, 14
Taxil, Leo (Gabriel Antoine Jogand), 174-175
Taylor, Zachary, 87
"Teapot Dome" scandal, 123
Tecumseh (Shooting Star), 67
Templars, Knights, 3, 9

Temple Lodge No. 247, Florida, 126
10,000 Famous Freemasons, 91
Tennessee, 90
Tennessee, Grand Lodge of, 67, 68, 70
"Tenure in Office Act". 103
Territory of New Mexico, 106
Texas, Grand Lodge of, 79, 80
Texas, Republic of, 79, 80
Thayer, John, 2
38th Foot, 86
Thomas, John, 2
Three Distinct Knocks, 78
Three Tuns, Lodge at the, 25
Thurmond, J. Strom, 144, 151
Tiber River, 7
Ticonderoga, 48
"Time Immemorial", 5, 34
"Tin Pan Alley", 124
Tippecanoe, Battle of, 67
Tokyo Bay, Japan, 141
Tombstone, Arizona, 112
Toombs, Robert, 91
Toronto, University of, viii
Torres, 52
Townshend Acts, 43
Training Camp Activities, Committee on, 120
Travis, William B., 80
"Treaty of Ghent", 68
Trenton Lodge No. 9, New Jersey, 58
Trenton, New Jersey, 46-47
trestle board, 179
Tribune, New York, 91
Trinity Church, Rhode Island, 40
Trinity College, Ireland, 5
Tripoli, 66
"Truman Doctrine", 144
Truman, Harry S., 70, 118, 119, quoted 129, 139; 132, 137, 140, 141, 143, 144, 145, 152-153, 154, 172
Tucker, P.C., 96
Tucson Lodge, Arizona, 112
Twain, Mark (Samuel L. Clemens), 101
200 Years, 119
"Typographical error", 170
Tyre, King's son of, 5
Unanimity Lodge No. 7, 53
Uncle Tom's Cabin, 88
Union Lodge No. 5, Delaware, 37
Union Lodge No. 7, Kansas, 134
Union Lodge, England, 18
Union of English Grand Lodges, 26-27

Union Pacific Railroad, 110
United Daughters of the Confederacy, 96
United Lodge No. 8, Maine, 98
United States Capitol, 63
United States of America, 39, 48, 52, 55, 56, 90, 105, 117, 124, 146
United States (frigate), 64
Unity Lodge No. 18, I.C., 44
Unity No. 18, Lodge of, 50
Upton, William, 164
Utah Territory, 105
Utah, Grand Lodge of, 105-106
Utah, Grand Lodge of, 80
Valley Forge, 48, 49
Van Devanter, Willis, 72
Van Rensselaer, Gen. Stephen, 40, 67
Vanguard, H.M.S., 25
Vaughan, Harry H., 145
"Vaughan, Miss Diana", 175
Vermont, 65, 124, 127, 146
Vermont, Grand Lodge of, 47, 65, 75
Veterans Affairs for the Veterans Administration, 143
Veterans' Administration Hospitals, 137, 139
Vice Presidents of the U.S. who were Freemasons, 148
Vichy government (France), 133
Vicksburg, Mississippi, 97
Victory Monument, Yorktown, Virginia, 111
Vietnam "Police Action", 67, 153
vigilantes, 173-174
Vincennes No.1, 167
Vincennes, Indiana, 49
Vinson, Frederick M., 72
Virginia City Lodge, 173
Virginia Craftsmen, 112
Virginia Gazette, 35
Virginia, 8, 35, 43, 49, 54, 57, 59, 60, 146
Virginia, Grand Lodge of, viii, 8, 47, 49, 52, 56, 57, 62, 65-66, 87, 102, 111, 149, 161, 181
von Steuben, Friedrich Wilhelm, 47, 49, 51, 52
Voorhis, Harold V.B., 152, 171
Vrooman, John Black, 142
Wabash River, 49
Waddall, Dewey W., 153
Wadsworth, Ebenezer, 83
Wainwright, Gen. Jonathan M., 134
Wainwright, I.W., 96

Walker, Walton H., 144
Walla Walla, Washington, 164
Wallace, George C., 151, 181
Wallace, Henry A., 144
Wallace, Lewis (Lew), 98, 125
Walter Reed Hospital, 118
Walter, Rev. William, 39
Walton, George, 53
War Department, 131
War for am ind, 152, 156
War for American Independence (Revolution), 39, 40, 43, 49, 53-54
War of 1812, 67-68, 73
War, declaration of, 118
Warm Springs, Georgia, 137
Warren Lodge No. 17, New York, 60
Warren, Dr. Joseph, 44
Warren, Earl, 72, 133, 147
Washington Lodge No. 1, Delaware, 37
Washington Times, The, 162
Washington, D.C., 81
Washington, George, 35-36, 39, 44, 46-47, 48, 49, 51, 53, 54, quoted, 55; 57, 58, 61, 62, 63, 64, 87, 90, 117, 163
Washington, Grand Lodge of, 86, 90, 157, 160, 163, 164
"Watergate", 153
Webb, Thomas Smith, 69, 78-79, 84-85
Weeton, George, 52
Wells, Lee E., 142
West Point Lodge No. 877, New York, 134, 144
West Point, New York, 48, 91
West Virginia, 85
West Virginia, Grand Lodge of, 102
Western Star Chapter No. 35, RAM, 73
Western Star Lodge No. 98, Missouri, 85
Wharton, Duke of, 17
Whipple, William, 53
White House (President's House), 145
White Plains, New York, 51
Who is Who in Freemasonry, 181
Widow's Son Lodge No. 60, Virginia, 112
Wilkes, John, 43
Williamette Lodge No. 2, Oregon, 92
Williamsburg Lodge No. 6, Virginia, 41, 62
Williamsburg, 52
Wilmington, Delaware, 37
Wilmington, North Carolina, 34
Wilson, Woodrow, 117, 120, 123
Winchester Hiram Lodge No. 21,

Virginia, 95, 102, 113
Winder Lodge No. 53, Georgia, 147
Winona (gunboat), 93
Wirt, William, 43
Wisconsin, Grand Lodge of, 79, 80, 163
Wood, Leonard C., 114
Woodbury, Levi, 72
Woodford, William, 52
Woods, William B., 72
Wooster, David, 40
World War I, 119, 144
World War II, 64, 80, 117, 119, 142, 144, 181
Wounded Knee, Battle of, 125
Wren Constitutions, 7
Wren, Sir Christopher, 3, 10
Wyler, William, 125
Wyoming, Grand Lodge of, 106
York chalice, 14
York Grand Lodge, 19
York Lodge No. 236, 18
York Lodge, 13, 17, 18
York Minster, 6
York Minster, fabric rolls, 14
York, England, 14
York, No. 1, Manuscript, 13
York, No. 2, Manuscript, 13
Yorktown Lodge No. 9, Virginia, 52
Yorktown, Virginia, 51, 52, 111
Young Mens Christian Association (YMCA), 119
Young, Brigham, 80, 105
Your Son is My Brother (film), 131
youth and Freemasonry, 178
Zanuck, Darryl, 146
Zetland, Marquis of, 15
Ziegfeld Follies, 126